JUDAISM

Keith Kahn-Harris

ALL THAT MATTERS

D1316870

Hodder Education
338 Euston Road, London NW1 3BH

Hodder Education is an Hachette UK company.

First published in UK 2012 by Hodder Education

First published in US 2012 by The McGraw-Hill Companies, Inc.

British Library Cataloguing in Publication Data: a catalogue record for this title is available from the British Library.

Library of Congress Catalog Card Number: on file.

10 9 8 7 6 5 4 3 2

The publisher has used its best endeavours to ensure that any website addresses referred to in this book are correct and active at the time of going to press. However, the publisher and the author have no responsibility for the websites and can make no guarantee that a site will remain live or that the content will remain relevant, decent or appropriate.

The publisher has made every effort to mark as such all words which it believes to be trademarks. The publisher should also like to make it clear that the presence of a word in the book, whether marked or unmarked, in no way affects its legal status as a trademark.

Every reasonable effort has been made by the publisher to trace the copyright holders of material in this book. Any errors or omissions should be notified in writing to the publisher, who will endeavour to rectify the situation for any reprints and future editions.

Hachette UK's policy is to use papers that are natural, renewable and recyclable products and made from wood grown in sustainable forests. The logging and manufacturing processes are expected to conform to the environmental regulations of the country of origin.

www.hoddereducation.co.uk

Typeset by Cenveo Publisher Services.

Printed and bound by CPI Group (UK) Ltd, Croydon, CR0 4YY

Contents

1	Introduction	1
2	Judaism on one foot	9
3	Jewish time	23
4	Living Jewishly	33
5	From Diaspora to emancipation	45
6	Divisions	57
7	Anti-Semitism	73
8	The Shoah and anti-Semitism today	83
9	The state of Israel	97
10	The Jewish people today and tomorrow	115
	Appendix: 100 Ideas	127
	Notes	145
	Acknowledgements and Picture credits	152
	Index	153

Introduction

It says 'Judaism' on the front of this book and perhaps you were expecting a book that explains the Jewish religion: what Jews believe, what they do in synagogue, what rituals they practise. But a book on the Jewish religion alone would be selling you short. This is a book about *the Jewish people* – and the Jewish people, with their long history and diversity, are bigger than the sum total of Jews' beliefs and rituals. Not all Jews share a common belief system and not all are religiously practising. So this book will discuss the Jewish religion but it will also do more, covering aspects of Jewish life that do not easily fit under the category of 'religion', such as Jewish history, politics, identity and culture.

▶ Who are the Jews?

There are estimated to be around 13.5 million Jews in the world today. This is a tiny number compared to the world's roughly 1.25 billion Muslims and 2 billion Christians. Outside of Israel, Jews do not form more than 2 per cent of any one country's population. Yet this modestly sized people contains extraordinary diversity and vitality.

So who are the Jews? On one level, the question is easy to answer: according to Jewish religious law, a Jew is someone who was born to a Jewish mother or has converted to Judaism. Today, though, some Jewish denominations also accept the child of a Jewish father as Jewish. Jews are sometimes defined by even more

▲ The Jewish people are a diverse people: an African woman prays
at the Western Wall in Jerusalem.

'lenient' criteria. The Nazis counted anyone with a Jewish
grandparent as Jewish, regardless of their current
religion. The state of Israel's Law of Return accepts as
eligible for Israeli citizenship a child or grandchild of a

Jew, the spouse of a Jew and the spouse of a child or grandchild of a Jew, but does not accept any Jew who has converted to another religion.

Of course, not everyone who is Jewish according to any of these criteria necessarily defines themselves as Jewish. To make things even more complicated, conversion to Judaism has always been possible and the descendants of converts are counted as Jewish in perpetuity. Different denominations today have different conversion standards and not all of them are recognized universally.

So not everyone who identifies themselves as Jewish is recognized by all other Jews as Jewish and not everyone who others define as Jewish identify as Jewish. Defining Jews can be a fraught process.

Connections: The term 'Jew'

The English word 'Jew' derives from the Latin term *Iudaeum*, meaning 'from Judea'. The Hebrew term for Jew, *Yehudi*, also meaning 'from Judea', appears in the biblical book of Esther. Judea is the southern part of the biblical land of Israel that was later to be ruled by the Romans, originally named after the tribe of Judah. The Bible also uses the term *Yisrael* (literally 'struggles with God') – Israel – to describe the Jews. In Genesis 32 Jacob's name is changed to Yisrael after he wrestles with God. The people of Yisrael are his descendants.

It's less problematic to define Jews in a light-hearted way. There are plenty of jokes Jews tell to sum up the Jewish experience. One is that the entire history of the Jewish people can be summed up as 'they tried to kill us, they failed, let's eat'. This joke plays on the remarkable fact of Jewish survival through the ages, despite massacres and expulsions, together with the centrality of food in Jewish life.

Another Jewish joke goes like this: Two Jews are shipwrecked on a desert island. A year later a ship comes to pick them up and finds three synagogues. The ship captain asks one of the Jews why there are three synagogues and he answers: 'One for him, one for me and one that neither of us would be seen dead going into.' Jews are a disputatious bunch.

▶ This book

This book introduces readers to Judaism, Jews and Jewishness. Chapters 2 to 4 survey the principal aspects of Judaism as a religion and a way of life. Chapters 5 to 7 explore the history of the Jewish Diaspora and how the emancipation of Jews in the Enlightenment created religious and political divisions within the Jewish people. Chapters 7 and 8 discuss the history of anti-Semitism, the *Shoah* (Holocaust) and contemporary anti-Semitism. Chapter 9 looks at the modern state of Israel and its impact on modern Jewish life. The final chapter discusses the Jewish people today, Jewish culture and its impact on the wider world, and what the future of the Jewish people might be.

There are a number of themes that will recur throughout this book:

1 Judaism is complicated.

Judaism is more than 3,000 years old and over time it has developed a huge body of practices. Jews have been scattered across the world and developed many different perspectives on what Judaism should consist of.

2 Judaism changed radically following the destruction of the Second Temple in 70 CE.

In ancient times, Jewish practice centred on sacrifices and rituals carried out at the Temple in Jerusalem. The destruction of the Second Temple by the Romans signalled the loss of Jewish political sovereignty and accelerated the dispersal of Jews across the world. Judaism adapted to become a 'portable' religion.

3 Judaism changed radically following emancipation in the 18th century.

From the late 18th century Jews in the Western world were gradually given the freedom to participate fully as citizens within their 'host' societies. This unprecedented freedom presented Judaism with new challenges.

4 Contemporary Judaism is highly diverse.

Following emancipation, many different approaches to Judaism have emerged. Particularly important is the distinction between 'Orthodox' Judaism that affirms a traditional view of the eternal validity of Jewish law, given by God to Moses, and 'Reform' and other non-Orthodox Judaisms that see Jewish traditions as subject to change and reinterpretation.

▶ A note on further reading

This book covers a huge amount of ground and will provide concise summaries of highly complex issues. Hopefully, readers will be sufficiently tantalized by what they read to investigate further. The '100 Ideas' section at the back of the book will list books and other sources that cover issues in more detail. At the end of the book you will find notes providing to references to sources that cannot be found in the 100 Ideas. Note number indicators are not used in the text; however, sources can be found in the notes by searching by chapter and quotation of the relevant passage.

A note on Hebrew

There is no standard way of transliterating Hebrew. I have made use of some of the most common transliterations, but readers should be aware that they may find other versions in other books and online. It may also help to know that the suffixes *-im* and *-ot* denote plurals, although I have tried to use the singular wherever possible.

Judaism on One Foot

The Talmud, one of Judaism's foundational books, tells the following tale:

> *Once, a certain gentile came before Rabbi Shammai and asked him: 'Take me as a proselyte, but on condition that you teach me the entire Torah all of it, while I stand on one foot.' Shammai instantly drove him away with a builder's measuring rod he happened to have in his hand. When the gentile came before Rabbi Hillel, Hillel said to him: 'What is hateful to you, do not do to your fellow man. That is the entire Torah, all of it, the rest is commentary. Go and study it.'*

Hillel is telling the prospective convert that the fundamental core of Judaism is an ethical message of dealing fairly with others. Notice that he doesn't mention God or belief. Rather it is *practice* that is central to Hillel's Judaism.

Hillel asks only one thing of the prospective convert: to 'go and learn it'. This demonstrates how central study is to Judaism.

So, by attempting in this chapter to teach Judaism 'on one foot', I am suggesting what Hillel suggested: this is just a start; go and study.

▶ Biblical Judaism

Let us start with Judaism as described in the Hebrew Bible. One can think of the biblical account of the Jewish people as a series of stages:

1 The world is created. Adam and Eve are expelled from Eden, humans people the earth, the world is nearly destroyed in the Flood with a remnant saved by Noah, the peoples of the world are scattered after the attempt to build the tower of Babel. (Genesis 1–11)

2 Abraham and his descendants reject idol worship and make a covenant with the one God. They become known as *Yisrael*. (Genesis 12–36)

3 Jacob's grandson Joseph and his descendants move to Egypt to escape famine, initially prospering and eventually being enslaved. (Genesis 37 – Exodus 1)

4 Moses is born and God appears to him in a burning bush; he approaches Pharaoh to let the Israelites leave. The Egyptians suffer ten plagues after which the Israelites escape, crossing the Red Sea into the desert. (Exodus 2–17)

5 The covenant between Israel and God is made, the Ten Commandments and the corpus of Jewish law is given on Mount Sinai, the land of Canaan is promised to Israel and the Ark of the Covenant is constructed. The generation that left Egypt, including Moses, is not allowed to enter the future land of Israel, so Israel wanders in the desert for 40 years. (Exodus, Leviticus, Numbers, Deuteronomy)

6 Under the leadership of Joshua, Israel enters and conquers Canaan, dividing the land between 12 tribes. Leadership passes from the 'judges' to a series of kings, starting with Saul. The Temple in Jerusalem is built by King Solomon. Through internal strife,

decadence and lack of faithfulness to God, Israel splits into two kingdoms – Judah and Israel. Israel is destroyed by the Assyrians in the 720 BCE, the ten resident tribes becoming 'lost' to history. Judah is conquered by the Babylonians in 587 BCE, its people are exiled and the Temple in Jerusalem is destroyed. (Joshua, Judges, Samuel and Kings)

7 Israel is exiled in Babylonia until the Persian King Cyrus allows them to return. The Temple in Jerusalem is rebuilt around 516 BCE. (Ezra, Chronicles)

The Hebrew Bible ends there but we can continue the story a little further:

8 A series of Jewish states, centred round the Temple in Jerusalem, exists in the land of Israel. They are subject to Persian, Greek, then Roman domination. Rebellions and civil wars are endemic. The Temple is destroyed by the Romans in 70 CE.

How accurate is this story? The early history of the Jews is obscure. In broad terms, the Bible coincides with the historical record more closely as it goes along. There is no evidence that Abraham, Jacob or Moses ever existed and the historicity of later kings such as Solomon is uncertain. There are no remains of the First Temple (although most scholars believe it existed), but the Second Temple definitely existed.

However, in its broad sweep the biblical narrative is accurate in that it tells the story of a set of tribes and kinship groups who over time coalesce into a people with a strong identity. The Jews emerged towards the end of the second millennium BCE as one of a number of tribes and early states in the general area of modern Israel. Judaism became centred on Jerusalem, reputedly founded as a capital of a united kingdom of Israel by King David around 1000 BCE, the location of the First and Second Temple. At the heart of the Temple was the *Kodesh Hakodashim*, the 'Holy of Holies', in which resided the Ark of the Covenant, a chest reputedly containing the tablets of the Ten Commandments. Jewish practice revolved around a complex series of sacrificial rituals conducted by the *Cohanim*, the priests. Judaism was a heterogeneous set of evolving myths and practices, until in the Babylonian exile of the 6th century BCE they were worked into a coherent religious system, bound together by the biblical text.

The Bible and subsequent Jewish texts see Judaism as the first *monotheism* – the doctrine that there is only one God – and the patriarch Abraham as the first monotheist and the first Jew. Although monotheism is not as historically unique as Jewish texts might have it – Zoroastrianism predates Judaism and has monotheistic elements – the purity and fervour of Judaism's monotheism *was* novel.

The Jewish God is not easy to live with. God describes itself as 'jealous' (Exodus 20: 5) and it is capable of cruel, arbitrary and even capricious acts. The patriarchs in the biblical texts give as good as they get: Jacob wrestles with it, Moses argues with it. This is a very personal God. At the same time, God is also immense in its oneness and omnipotence. It expresses its essence in impossible riddles as when it tells Moses, 'I am that I am' (Exodus 3:

14). God's true name is a mystery: a combination of the Hebrew letters YHVH whose correct pronunciation was only known to the High Priest of the Temple (and then only spoken, in private, once a year).

God is immensely demanding, requiring Jews to separate themselves from other peoples. The separateness that God demands is part of the *Brit* (covenant) made with a number of the patriarchs in the Bible. Abraham is promised to be the father of a great nation (Genesis 12–17) and his descendants are to be circumcised as a sign of this covenant. The covenant is passed on to Isaac, Jacob/Israel, Joseph and Ephraim. The covenant is elaborated in the giving of the Torah to the Jewish people at Mount Sinai (Exodus 19–24). Israel is to be God's chosen people if they keep its laws. The rewards for this would be in both this life, with a productive land for the Jews, but also in the next one (although the rewards here are very non-specific).

Connections: The Noachide Laws

Being chosen does not mean that Jews are superior to other people. After the Flood, God promised not to destroy the earth again in a covenant made with Noah. Since all people are seen as descendants of Noah, the so-called 'Noachide Laws' apply to all. These laws include prohibitions on murder, theft and idolatry but are much less demanding than the laws that God requires the Jews alone to obey.

Judaism is sometimes thought of as a 'particularist' religion, concerned with Jews above all else. But Judaism also has 'universalist' tendencies, with a strong ethical component – it is sometimes described as 'ethical monotheism' – and many laws governing relations between Jews and non-Jews. God warns Israel not to 'oppress the stranger' (Exodus 23: 9). *Tzedakah* or charity is a core value of Judaism and its recipients are not restricted to Jews alone.

Life is God's supreme gift and its preservation is vital to ethical behaviour. In Jewish law, the concept of *Pikuach Nefesh* (saving of life) holds that virtually any commandment can be broken to preserve a life. Pleasure in this world – including sexual pleasure – is to be enjoyed, provided it is pleasure governed by the boundaries of Jewish law.

Life is also filled with pain, suffering and evil, which entered the world following Adam and Eve's fall. Humans are born morally neutral, but endowed with an evil inclination (*yetzer hara*) and a good inclination (*yetzer tov*). The fate of individuals is in their own hands and repentance (*teshuvah*) is always possible.

Judaism also has an eye on the future. Jewish thinking is unclear on what awaits the dead, but they will be judged on their past lives; the righteous ones entering *Haolam Haba* (the world to come) and the wicked punished. At some point, the *Moshiach* (Messiah), a descendant of King David, will gather in the exiled Jewish people to the land of Israel. The dead will be resurrected and the world will be perfected with all of humanity sharing in the messianic age.

▶ The people of the book

Jews are sometimes referred to as 'the people of the book'. There is no one 'book' though; rather Judaism has a collection of canonical texts. The most important include:

▶ **Torah (teaching):** The first five books of the Hebrew Bible:

  ▶ *Bereshit* ('In the beginning', known as Genesis in English)

  ▶ *Shemot* ('Names', known as Exodus)

  ▶ *Vayikra* ('And he called', known as Leviticus)

  ▶ *Bamidbar* ('In the wilderness', known as Numbers)

  ▶ *Devarim* ('Words', known as Deuteronomy).

These books cover the period from the creation of the world to the eve of the entry into the Promised Land. Traditionally, the entirety of the Torah is read aloud in synagogue over the course of each year, with sections read each Sabbath. The Torah is read from a parchment scroll, the *sefer Torah* that is still today written by hand with a quill pen.

▶ **Tanakh:** The entire Hebrew Bible, containing the following sections:

  ▶ *Torah* (see above)

  ▶ *Neviim* ('prophets'): Eight books (Joshua, Judges, 1 and 2 Samuel, 1 and 2 Kings, together with the major and minor prophets) telling the story of Israel from entry into Canaan to the Babylonian exile. It includes books by prophets such as Isaiah and Jeremiah chastising the Jewish people for the misdeeds that led to the exile and holding out hope of a return to the land.

▶ *Ketuvim* ('writings'): Eleven further books, some of which are historical and others in various genres.

▶ **Talmud (instruction/learning):** An enormous edited record of rabbinic discussions, written largely in Aramaic, recording and expanding existing oral traditions. Although primarily dedicated to the exposition of Jewish law, it also includes discussion of theology, philosophy and lore. There are two versions – the Jerusalem, completed about 400 CE and the Babylonian, completed about 500 CE. The latter is used more frequently today. The Talmud consists of the following elements:

▶ *Mishnah*: Redacted by Rabbi Judah HaNasi in about 200 CE and written mostly in Hebrew. Its six tractates record and summarize the oral debates of the rabbis subsequent to the destruction of the Second Temple.

▶ *Gemara*: The expansion of the Mishnah by rabbis in Israel and Babylonia, written mostly in Aramaic. Since the advent of printing, each individual page of the Talmud usually consists of the Mishnah and Gemara in a central column, with the medieval commentaries of the rabbi Rashi (in a special script) on a thin column next to the inner margin and those of the rabbis known as the Tosafists next to the outer margin. Particular editions will also include other marginal commentaries and glosses on the same page.

ארבעה

▲ A page of the Talmud: the Mishnah and Gemara are in the centre, surrounded by commentaries.

Judaism on One Foot

The Talmud is a highly challenging 'book'. It is long (500 chapters over multiple volumes), but stylistically terse. There is no narrative and no clear summaries of the dense discussions.

▶ **Midrash:** A method of biblical exegesis, using a number of interpretive tools to draw out the Bible's hidden meanings and lessons. Its form is sometimes deceptively simple, including parables and stories. There are a number of compilations of Midrash, the best known being *Midrash Rabbah* which expounds a number of books of the Bible.

▶ **Responsa and codes:** The voluminous nature of the Jewish canon gave rise to the need for explicit rulings on matters of Jewish law and practice. There is a large literature of 'responsa': answers by prominent rabbis, to legal or theological questions. There have also been attempts to codify Jewish law, such as the medieval scholar Maimonides' *Mishneh Torah* and Joseph Caro's *Shulchan Aruch*, a 1565 guide to Jewish law and practice that has proved to be highly influential up until the present day.

▶ **Kabbalah:** The Jewish esoteric tradition, reflecting on the nature of God and the universe. Traditionally, Kabbalistic thinking was practised by elite Jewish thinkers only, sometimes secretly, and rarely written down. In the second millennia CE, knowledge of Kabbalh has spread, assisted by medieval works such as the *Zohar*.

Hebrew is the language of the Bible and of much Jewish prayer. A Semitic language, it is written from left to right in a consonant-only script of 22 letters. Hebrew was the spoken language in ancient Israel until at least the Babylonian exile and probably several centuries after, too. Thereafter, it continued as a written and ritual language until modern times. Aramaic, the lingua franca of the ancient Middle East, gradually supplanted Hebrew as an everyday language until long after the destruction of the Second Temple. Jews write Aramaic in the same alphabet as Hebrew and the two languages are closely related.

In Jewish tradition, the Torah was revealed by God to Moses on Mount Sinai, in two parts: the written Torah and the oral Torah. The latter was passed on from Moses through the generations until its written exposition in the Talmud. Modern biblical scholarship has made such beliefs difficult to sustain empirically. The Torah was edited together over time through the work of a number of authors, who probably drew on existing oral traditions. It also draws on a substrate of older Middle Eastern mythology (for example, there is a catastrophic flood in the Babylonian epic of *Gilgamesh*, dating to the early part of the 2nd millennium BCE).

While Jewish tradition sees the Torah as divine, it is not fixed and unchanging. A remarkable story in the Babylonian Talmud illustrates the importance of interpretation. It concerns a discussion regarding whether a particular kind of oven is ritually pure or impure:

On that day, Rabbi Eliezer bought forward every imaginable argument, but the sages did not accept any of them. Finally he said to them, 'If the Halachah agrees with me, let this carob tree prove it!' Sure enough, the carob tree was uprooted [and replanted] one hundred cubits away from its place. 'No proof can be brought from a carob tree,' they retorted.

Again he said to them, 'If the Halachah agrees with me, let the channel of water prove it!' Sure enough, the channel of water flowed backward. 'No proof can be brought from a channel of water,' they rejoined.

Again he urged, 'If the Halachah agrees with me, let the walls of the house of study prove it!' Sure enough, the walls tilted as if to fall. But Rabbi Joshua rebuked the walls, saying, 'When disciples of the wise are engaged in halachic dispute, what right have you to interfere?' Hence, in deference to Rabbi Joshua, they did not fall, and in deference to Rabbi Eliezer they did not resume their upright position, they are still standing aslant.

Again Rabbi Eliezer then said to the Sages, 'If the Halachah agrees with me, let it be proved from heaven!' Sure enough, a divine voice cried out, 'Why do you dispute Rabbi Eliezer with whom the Halachah always agrees?' Rabbi Joshua stood up and protested, 'The Torah is not in heaven' (Deuteronomy 30: 12). We pay no attention to a divine voice, because long ago, at Mount Sinai, You wrote in the Torah, 'After the majority must one incline' (Exodus 23:2).

Rabbi Nathan met [the prophet] Elijah and asked him, 'What did the Holy One do in that moment?' Elijah: 'He laughed, saying "My sons have defeated me, my sons have defeated me."'

The Torah is a continuing conversation, transmitted through study and debate. While there are boundaries beyond which traditionally minded Jews will rarely cross, such as questioning the existence of God, within these boundaries there is room for rigorous discussion and disagreement.

▶ *Halachah* and *mitzvot*

Judaism is bound together by *halachah*, literally translated as 'path' or 'way', but commonly understood as 'law'. Halachah emerges out of the 613 commandments given in the Torah and built on in the Talmud. There is virtually no area of human activity that halachah does not touch, from getting married to going to the toilet. Halachah contains a myriad of individual practices known as *mitzvot* (singular: *mitzvah*). A mitzvah is a commandment but it has also come to mean a moral act.

In the next two chapters I will describe some of the 'core' mitzvot. This doesn't mean that all Jews today follow all these practices, but at the very least 'Orthodox' Jews – whom we will discuss in more detail in Chapter 6 – do try to.

Jewish Time

Ancient Judaism was focused in *space*: while the Temple in Jerusalem stood, services and rituals were concentrated there, on the Holy of Holies, the seat of God's presence. In contrast, as the theologian Abraham Joshua Heschel argued, since the destruction of the Second Temple Jews have found holiness in *time*. Much of Jewish observance consists of marking out and sanctifying time on a number of scales:

▶ **Daily:** Prayer services take place three times a day – morning, afternoon and evening. Blessings are said before and after food and on many other occasions.

▶ **Weekly:** *Shabbat*, the Sabbath, is one of the most important Jewish rituals of all. Lasting from Friday to Saturday sunset, it marks God's resting on the seventh day of creation. As well as extended services to mark the day, there are prohibitions on doing any kind of work on Shabbat. These include not lighting a fire, which in the modern world has been understood to mean not turning on a light, cooking, driving or using the telephone. Shabbat commences in the home on Friday evenings with candle lighting and blessings over wine and bread (usually a platted loaf called *chollah*). It finishes on Saturday evening with a ceremony called *Havdalah*.

▶ **Monthly:** *Rosh Chodesh* (the new moon) is marked in the liturgy for the daily and Shabbat prayer services.

▶ **Yearly:** A number of festivals mark the passage of the year. Judaism operates on an adjusted lunar calendar which ensures that festivals tie in roughly with the seasons. Each festival has its unique rituals and many of them require the same prohibitions on work as on Shabbat. The main festivals are:

▶ *Rosh Hashanah*: the Jewish new year, in early autumn. It is a day of solemnity and reflection. The *shofar*, a hollowed-out ram's horn, is blown in synagogue, to commemorate the ram that Abraham sacrificed in Genesis 22. Honey-based foods are eaten to symbolize a sweet new year.

▶ *Yom Kippur*: the Day of Atonement, ten days after Rosh Hashanah. It is marked by a 25-hour fast and a day spent in prayer and collective repentance.

▶ *Sukkot*: an autumn harvest festival lasting seven days, in which Jews eat and sleep in a temporary structure called a *sukkah* to recall those the booths Jews slept in during their wanderings in Sinai.

▶ *Simchat Torah*: This follows directly on from Sukkot and celebrates the completion of the annual cycle of reading from the Torah. The last few verses of Deuteronomy and the first verses of Genesis are read. It is customary to dance and process with the Torah scroll in the synagogue.

▶ *Chanukah*: Celebrated in November/December over eight nights, Chanukah commemorates the rededication of the Second Temple after its despoiling by the Greeks during the Maccabean Revolt in the 2nd century BCE. According to later sources, one day's supply of oil for the eternal flame in the Temple lasted for eight. A nine-branched candleholder called a *chanukiah* is lit every night, one candle at a time. Oily foods such as doughnuts and potato pancakes (*latkah*) are eaten to commemorate the miracle of the oil.

▶ *Purim*: Celebrated in late winter, Purim commemorates the deliverance of the Jewish people from a plot by the Persian king's vizier Haman to kill the Jews, as recorded in the biblical book of Esther. It is marked by the reading of the book of Esther, drunkenness, fancy dress, skits and gift-giving.

▶ *Pesach*: A spring harvest festival which also marks the Exodus of Israel from Egypt. It lasts seven days during which leavened foods are not eaten to recall how Israel fled Egypt so fast that their bread did not have time to rise. Unleavened bread (*matzah*) is eaten to mark the festival. The first night of Pesach is marked by telling the story of the Exodus from Egypt at a *seder* meal, from a special book called a *Haggadah.*

▶ *Shavuot*: Seven weeks after Pesach, Shavuot commemorates both the harvest and the giving of the Torah at Mount Sinai. It is celebrated by the reading of the biblical book of Ruth, eating dairy produce and all-night Torah study.

▶ *Tisha B'Av*: A fast day held in summer, Tisha B'Av commemorates the destruction of both temples as well as a number of other catastrophes in Jewish history. The biblical book of Lamentations is read.

▶ There are also a number of other fasts and minor festivals, together with a series of time periods with their own customs and prohibitions such as the *Omer* (between Pesach and Shavuot) and the Ten Days of Repentance between Rosh Hashanah and Yom Kippur.

Connections: Modern Israeli festivals

Since Israel independence in 1948, four other secular holidays have been instituted which are observed in Israel and to varying degrees in the Diaspora: *Yom Ha'atzmaut* – Independence Day; *Yom HaShoah* – Holocaust Remembrance Day; *Yom Hazikaron* – Memorial Day; *Yom Yerushalayim* – Jerusalem Day.

▶ **Life cycle events:** A Jew's life is structured by a number of key milestones. The main ones are:

   ▶ *Brit milah*: Jewish boys are circumcised, ideally on the eighth day after birth, as a sign of the covenant (brit) between God and Israel.

   ▶ *Simchat bat*: a modern celebration for the birth of a girl.

   ▶ *Bar/Bat mitzvah*: a ceremony held at age 13 to mark a child's coming of age and responsibility for their own religious actions. In synagogue, the bar mitzvah is called to give the blessing over the Torah and to read a portion from it. Traditionally, only boys had bar mitzvahs but in recent decades non-Orthodox movements have instituted *bat* mitzvahs in which girls do the same as boys.

   ▶ *Chupah* (marriage): Marriages were traditionally arranged (and still are in ultra-Orthodox communities) but both parties must consent. Marriage is accorded great value in Judaism but divorce (called a *get*) is permitted. There are a number of stages in a Jewish marriage, culminating in *erusin* (sanctification), in which the marriage contract (*ketubah*) is signed and the *hatan* (groom) gives a ring to the *kallah* (bride) and *nissuin*, the marriage ceremony itself (which today immediately follows *erusin* but in pre-modern times could follow up to a year after), held under a canopy (*chupah*) with seven special blessings being recited over the couple.

▶ **Death:** Following death, burial (*levayah*) ideally takes place within 24 hours. The body is prepared by a *chevrah kadisha* ('holy society') who ritually purify the body and dress it in white. Jewish cemeteries tend to be austere places, with stones placed on graves rather than flowers. The mourners (children, parents, brothers, sisters and spouses of the deceased) recite the *kaddish* prayer over the deceased at the cemetery and subsequently at various points throughout the mourning period (although in Orthodox communities women do not recite kaddish). The first seven days of the mourning period are known as *shiva* in which mourners sit on low chairs and do not work, bathe or shave. Following the shiva there are further mourning periods of 30 days and one year, each with their own rituals. The anniversary of the death (sometimes called *yartzheit*) is marked annually by the lighting of a candle and special prayers.

▶ Jewish prayer

Tefillah (prayer) began to develop in Temple times and a few key prayers date from this era. With the destruction of the Second Temple, the importance of prayer increased

▲ An unfurled Torah scroll, surrounded by decorative crown, breastplate and other accoutrements.

and the liturgy expanded and became standardized. Towards the end of the first millennium CE, *siddurim* (prayer books) started to be compiled.

Although synagogue prayer leaders recite some prayers on behalf of the congregation, they are in no sense an intermediary between the Jews and God. Three-times daily prayers can be recited in a few minutes but Shabbat and festival services, particularly the morning service, can last over three hours in some synagogues. In Orthodox synagogues virtually the entire service is recited in Hebrew. In non-Orthodox synagogues, more of the vernacular is used.

Jewish liturgy is not confined to the simple reading of prayers. Prayer is often chanted, and some sections of the liturgy, particularly those based on Psalms, hymns or poems, are sung. Shabbat, festivals and some other services include readings from the Torah and from the biblical books of the prophets. Sermons and learned addresses often punctuate the service. Some services include other rituals such as dressing and undressing the Torah scroll and processing it around the synagogue, lighting candles and blessing wine.

There are a number of 'core' prayers that occur in most services. Three particularly important ones are:

▶ **The Shema:** Judaism's most important prayer. It encapsulates the stark monotheistic beliefs at the heart of Judaism, together with the importance of mitzvot. It is recited in morning and evening prayers and on going to sleep. Its opening verses are traditionally recited on one's deathbed.

▶ **The Amidah:** A series of 19 blessings, recited three times a day and on various other occasions in various different forms. The Amidah forms the kernel around which the rest of the service revolves. It is said standing (*amidah* means 'standing' in Hebrew), ideally facing Jerusalem.

▶ **Kaddish:** an Aramaic prayer that sanctifies God's name. It is recited on completing a section of the service and a version of the Kaddish is recited by mourners during the year-long mourning period and on the anniversary of the death.

Connections: More on the Shema

The Shema consists of three sections of the Torah (Deuteronomy 6: 4–9 and 11: 13–21 and Numbers 15: 37–41) that begin with the declaration: 'Hear, O Israel: the Lord is our God, the Lord is one.' It commands Jews to 'love the Lord your God with all your heart, with all your soul and with all your might', to remember these words, to teach them to one's children, to recite them twice a day, and to bind them as a sign on one's hands and head and to fix them to the doorpost. The second section of the Shema declares that obeying God's commandments will lead to the reward of a plentiful harvest and disobeying will lead to punishment. The third section commands the wearing of *tzitzit* 'that you may remember and do all my commandments, and be holy unto your God'.

Prayer in Judaism serves a number of purposes. It is a form of discipline intended to intensify one's commitment to God and mitzvot. It should ideally be conducted with *kavanah*, or sincere intention. It is a way of meeting and even unifying with God (*devekut*). It is a form of supplication, intended to demonstrate one's worthiness for good things to happen. It is an affirmation of community – prayer ideally takes place within a *minyan*, a quorum of ten adult Jewish males (although non-Orthodox denominations today count women as part of a minyan). Prayer can take place anywhere, but the synagogue has become the paramount setting for Jewish prayer. The word 'synagogue' derives from the Greek word for 'assembly' and it is known in Hebrew as *beit knesset* (house of assembly).

Connections: The synagogue

Synagogues differ widely in size – from one-room *shteibls* used by ultra-Orthodox Jews to the imposing 'temples' of American Reform Judaism. There are some features common to most synagogues: a raised *bimah* (dias) from which the Torah is read, an *aron kodesh* (ark/cabinet) in which the Torah scrolls are kept, traditionally facing towards Jerusalem, and a *ner tamid* (perpetual light), a lamp to remind Jews of the Menorah in the Temple. In Orthodox synagogues, women are confined to a separate section or a gallery. The synagogue is also a place of study and a community centre, and today they may be used for activities as diverse as classes for children, youth clubs, soup kitchens and weddings.

Living Jewishly

Judaism is highly concerned with boundaries: between Jews and other peoples, between Jewish and non-Jewish time, between Jewish and non-Jewish space, between Jews and other Jews. A number of practices are particularly important in creating these boundaries:

▶ **Shabbat and festivals**: The rigorous strictures against any kind of work on Shabbat and festivals ensure that observant Jews will be separated from their non-Jewish neighbours in certain respects. For example, observant Jews will not be able to work in shops or markets that open on Saturday. In the modern age they will need to live close to their synagogues as they will not be able to use a car.

▶ **Sexuality:** Judaism accords no value to celibacy. However, traditionally sex has to take place between a man and a woman within marriage. Women who are in *niddah* (a state of ritual impurity during menstruation or after childbirth) are not allowed to touch or have sex with their husbands, until they have bathed in the *mikveh*, the ritual bath. These laws are not observed by most non-Orthodox Jews.

▶ **Endogamy:** Although there is no Jewish law against marriage with non-Jews, there is a strong preference for marriage between Jews. Even non-Orthodox denominations today favour endogamy, or at least conversion of a non-Jewish spouse.

▶ *Kashrut***:** The intricate Jewish dietary laws determine what foods are deemed 'fit' (the literal meaning of kashrut). The laws of kashrut are set out in the

Bible, but have been considerably elaborated since then. Cooking and eating utensils are rendered non-kosher through contact with forbidden foods, although they can be made kosher through specified cleaning processes. Those who keep strictly kosher will only eat food whose provenance they are absolutely sure of and will only use restaurants that are certified as kosher by a reputable Jewish authority.

Connections: The main points of kashrut

▶ Mammals must be vegetarian, chew the cud and have cloven hooves.

▶ Birds of prey and shellfish are forbidden.

▶ All reptiles are forbidden as are all insects, except for some species of locust.

▶ Fish must have scales and fins.

▶ Meat and milk must not be eaten in the same dish or at the same meal.

▶ Mammals and birds must be slaughtered by a method called *shechita*, in which the animal is killed through cutting the throat with a sharp knife.

▶ Certain parts of the animal's body, such as the sciatic nerve, together with blood, have to be removed before eating.

▶ Wine and some other products need to be prepared by Jews to be kosher.

- **Dress:** While most contemporary Jews usually dress the same as their non-Jewish neighbours, many Orthodox Jews wear distinctive clothes. In addition, there are also various forms of dress used in prayer:

  - *Tzniut* (modesty): Modesty involves dressing in clothes that do not highlight the contours of the body and reveal excessive skin. For Orthodox Jewish women today, modesty means wearing long sleeves and long skirts.

  - Head covering: Married women are required to cover their hair in public. Men are required to cover their heads while praying but over time the custom developed for covering the head at all times. A *kippah* (skull cap) is worn at all times by Orthodox men, often with a hat on top. Non-Orthodox Jews usually wear a kippah during prayer and women are now doing so, too, in increasing numbers.

  - *Tallit* and *tzitzit*: The third paragraph of the Shema commands Jews to put *tzittzit* (fringes) on their garments. Over time this has formed the basis of two traditions. One is for men to wear an undershirt with long fringes; the other is to wear a shawl with fringes (*tallit*) during prayer. The latter is common even among non-Orthodox Jews and is being increasingly adopted by women as well.

  - *Tefillin*: The Shema commands Jews to 'bind' its words on one's arm and between one's eyes. This has come to mean wearing *tefillin* – two small boxes containing biblical verses, bound on to the upper arm and the forehead using leather straps. Men

Living Jewishly

(and today some women, too) wear them during weekday morning prayers.

▶ *Shatnez*: The Bible prohibits wearing wool and linen in the same garment.

▶ Beards and *peyot*: Although the Bible prohibits cutting the corners of the head (of hair) and the beard, the ambiguity in the relevant verses has meant that Jewish law is not clear. Many Orthodox Jews today grow beards and some never trim them. Some sects do not cut a strip of hair above the ear, resulting in long ringlets called *peyot.*

▶ Clothing styles: Orthodox Jews often have distinctive dress styles. *Haredim* (see Chapter 6) often dress in ways derived from 18th-century Polish noblemen's styles – long black coats, knickerbockers, a broad-brimmed hat and, on Shabbat, a fur hat called a *streiml.*

▶ **Other markers of identity:** The doorposts of Jewish houses are marked with *mezuzot* – small boxes containing biblical verses – in fulfilment of a commandment given in the Shema. There are various other symbols of Judaism that may mark the bodies and homes of Jews, such as necklaces with a *Magen David* (Star of David) or a *chai* (the Hebrew word for 'life'). The seven-branch *menorah* (a kind of candelabra) also appears frequently in Jewish art.

It is difficult to practise Judaism on one's own. Some mitzvot, such as the preference for prayer within a minyan, explicitly require a community for them to be practised. When Jews settle in a new location, mikvot, cemeteries, slaughterhouses and synagogues are usually set up, together with welfare and other institutions.

The Jewish family is a building block of Jewish community. Within the family and the community at large, women, men and children have traditionally had different roles. Children and women are excused from many mitzvot – they are not counted as part of a minyan, for example. Jewish tradition has generally excluded women from leading prayers and acting and their primary responsibility was the domestic sphere. In modern times the Jewish attitude to women has been challenged by non-Orthodox Judaisms, most of which now accord women equal status. Even in contemporary Orthodoxy, women are more likely to be Jewishly educated than was previously the case. Homosexuality is now accepted in most non-Orthodox Judaisms, with same-sex marriages now carried out in many synagogues. Even if the concept of the Jewish family has been liberalized in some contemporary Judaisms, rituals such as lighting Shabbat candles and the Passover seder meal still rely on the family.

The centrality of family and community, the preference for endogamy, together with the demanding nature of Jewish practice, have all created strong boundaries between Jews and non-Jews. These boundaries have been further reinforced by a reluctance to seek converts. There were periods in antiquity when Jews proselytized; however, over time strong barriers to admitting potential converts have built up. In the Talmud, converts need to be authorized by a *Beth Din* (see below) and conversion requires immersion in the mikvah and circumcision for men. On top of these requirements, a tradition grew that converts should initially be refused, as a test of sincerity, and that conversion requires detailed knowledge of and commitment to Jewish religious practice. Orthodox conversions today remain demanding but non-Orthodox denominations have become more welcoming to potential converts.

Traditionally, a *Cohen* (descendant of the priestly caste) is not allowed to marry a divorcee or a convert. A child of certain forbidden relationships, such as the child of an adulterous woman or of incest, is known as a *mamzer* and can marry only converts or other mamzerim, a prohibition that is passed on to their children. A woman cannot divorce a man without his consent (although the reverse is possible) which sometimes leads to women becoming *agunot*, or 'chained', unable to remarry for an indefinite period of time. Most non-Orthodox Judaisms have now abandoned such practices as cruel or invalid in the modern world.

Since the destruction of the Second Temple, religious authority has rested with rabbis, who issue rulings on how halacha should be applied to particular cases. More contentious cases are heard in a Beth Din, usually consisting of three rabbis. The scope of and limits to a Beth Din or rabbi's authority vary greatly. A rabbi is simply someone whom another rabbi has ordained (through a ceremony known as *semicha*). Rabbis are ordained within a variety of seminaries, some of whose 'graduates' are not recognized as rabbis by other rabbis. Although there are no official gradations in rabbinic status, some rabbis are particularly revered for their learning and authority. In addition, some communities choose 'grand' or 'chief' rabbis to represent Jewish communities to the wider world.

▶ What do Jews actually believe?

The emphasis on 'doing' in Judaism means that individual Jews do not have to confront and affirm their beliefs with any regularity. Judaism does not require clear and unambiguous statements of faith. In Islam, the *Shahadah*, the declaration of faith in God and Mohammed as his prophet, has a central place in worship. Although the Shema comes close to this, it is still only one important prayer among others. Outside the Kabbalah, some forms of medieval Jewish philosophy and contemporary theology, Judaism has often avoided abstract theological discussions.

These caveats aside, probably the best-known statement of Jewish belief is the medieval Jewish thinker Maimonedes' Thirteen Principles of Faith, from his *Mishneh Torah* (see '100 Ideas' section at the back of the book). These principles describe reasonably accurately the 'core' of Orthodox Jewish doctrine today. Yet different movements and thinkers at different points in time and in different locations have emphasized particular aspects of Jewish belief. For example, some Jewish movements have been obsessed with preparing for the arrival of the Messiah.

Orthodox Jewish belief appears 'fundamentalist', as it is predicated on eternal truths embodied in divinely revealed scriptures. Jewish fundamentalism can have similar baleful effects to other fundamentalisms, such as the inflexible application of laws regardless of human consequences, the marginalization of women and homosexuals, and extremist nationalism.

Non-Orthodox Judaisms are more ready to challenge or adapt aspects of Jewish doctrine. Some have removed references to, for example, the rebuilding of the Temple from their liturgy. Traditional beliefs are sometimes reinterpreted in metaphorical ways, with, for example, belief in the coming of the Messiah transformed into a desire for a 'messianic age'.

On the question of God, both Orthodox and non-Orthodox Jews often share a haziness in describing what it is. This haziness doesn't necessarily imply doubt about God's existence; it is more a function of the ineffable nature of God. For some non-Orthodox Jews, though, this haziness is part of a non-literal understanding of God.

It is perfectly common for even contemporary Orthodox-practising Jews to be, if not atheists, then relatively unconcerned about the existence of God. The manifold practices and rituals that constitute Judaism can be fulfilling to perform for their own sake. That isn't to say that some unbelieving Jews don't also find Jewish practice pointless, but it is much more feasible to be a non-believing practising Jew than it is to be a non-believing practising Christian or Muslim.

Even the most traditionalist Judaisms can be remarkably elastic in some respects. Jewish textual interpretation distinguishes between different levels of meaning in the Bible with the most obvious (the *pshat*) being only the most simplistic. This has meant that some Orthodox Jews take a non-literal interpretation of the seven days of creation.

▶ What do Jews actually do?

Not all Jews practise Judaism in the same way. In the modern world Jewish practice is a kind of continuum. At one end are ultra-Orthodox Jews who try and perform as many mitzvot as possible and at the other are entirely secular Jews who keep no Jewish practices at all. Between the two poles, the majority of Jews come to some kind of accommodation with what they will and will not practise. There are some practices that are performed almost exclusively by Orthodox Jews, such as visiting the mikveh. There are some practices that even some Orthodox Jews do not perform, such as shatnes. There are also practices that even entirely secular Jews perform, such as the Passover seder.

▲ A family conducting a seder meal on Pesach. Women today do not always take such a passive role!

One of the remarkable things about contemporary Judaism is how many commitments even those who are lukewarm in their beliefs and identity will take on. Take an average 'moderately engaged' British Jew: most will circumcise their sons; send them to a Jewish day or Sunday school; fix a mezuzah to their homes; avoid pork and shellfish at home; join a synagogue and attend a couple of times a year at least; and organize a seder and fast on Yom Kippur.

5

From Diaspora to Emancipation

The destruction of the Second Temple in 70 BCE was a major turning point in Jewish history. Although Jews had lived outside the land of Israel even during Temple times, Jews now came to think of themselves as being 'in exile' (*galut*). Yearning and mourning for *Tzion* – Zion, the synonym for Jerusalem and the Temple – became an integral part of Jewish prayer. Even now there is a Jewish state, Judaism is indelibly marked by the practices and structures that developed in exile.

The post-exilic Jewish people formed a diaspora, a term deriving from the word for 'scattering' in the Greek translation of the Bible. Even 60 years after the modern state of Israel was refounded, nearly half of the Jewish people live in the Diaspora.

In the Diaspora, the customs of the Jews and the culture of different communities diversified. Some Diaspora communities became isolated from the main currents of Judaism and either withered over time or developed divergent forms of Judaism. The Jews of Ethiopia, for example, developed a different canon of holy books and a different set of festivals and holy days.

One of the most controversial questions regarding the Jewish people is to what extent today's Jews are the descendants of the ancient land of Israel. Writers such as Shlomo Sand have argued that the extent of post-exilic Jewish proselytization has been underestimated to the extent that it is problematic to talk of the historical continuity of the Jewish people. They point in particular to the conversion to Judaism of the Khazar people in the Caucuses in the 8th century CE as a possible origin of the large Eastern European Jewish population. The historical record is fragmentary and unclear, but it is certainly true that, at the very least in the ancient world, Jews did attract significant numbers of converts. Further, mixed marriages in which spouses became Jewish may also have been more common in the past, particularly in the first millennium CE. On the other hand, modern genetic studies do suggest a degree of common descent for much of the Jewish people, with Cohanim (Jews who claim descent from the Temple priesthood) showing strong signs of a common origin.

▶ The diversity of the Diaspora

There are three broad groups of Diaspora Jews, distinguished by customs, culture and language that endure, in part at least, to this day:

1 **Ashkenazi** Jews trace their origins to Eastern Europe, the Russian Empire and Germany. In particular, many of them are descendants of Jews who lived in the Pale of Settlement, a part of the western Russian Empire to which most Jews were confined from the late 18th century. In this area Jews were spread around hundreds of small towns with large or majority Jewish populations, known as *shtetls* – later immortalized (and sentimentalized) in the musical *Fiddler on the Roof*. The heartlands of Ashkenazi Jewry were decimated in the Holocaust, but by then a considerable number had moved to the English-speaking world, South America and Israel. Ashkenazi Jews remain the largest single group of Jews. In the second millennium CE, Ashkenazi Jews developed their own language, Yiddish, which is

based on German, but has been strongly influenced by Hebrew and various Eastern European languages. Today Yiddish is generally spoken as a native language only by ultra-Orthodox Jews.

2 **Sephardi** Jews are those who trace their origins to the Jews of Spain and Portugal, who were expelled in 1492. Salonika in Greece became the major Sephardi settlement, known as the 'Jerusalem of the Balkans'. Holland was also an important Sephardi centre. Salonikan Jewry was almost wiped out in the Holocaust and these days Sephardi Jews tend to form a minority within most Jewish communities. Sephardi Jews had their own language, Ladino, a form of early modern Spanish with influences from Hebrew and various other tongues, but this has largely died out as a living language.

3 **Mizrachi** Jews come from 'eastern' societies, particularly the Arab and Islamic world (including North Africa). Jews formed a significant and long-established proportion of Arab cities such as Cairo, Baghdad and Damascus. Following the establishment of the state of Israel, most Mizrachi Jews emigrated to Israel, either through choice or force. Small Mizrachi Jewish communities remain in Iran, Morocco and Tunisia. Some Mizrachi Jews spoke Judeo-Arabic, a language that has largely died out.

Connections: Jews who don't fit

There are Jews who are neither Ashkenazi, Sephardi nor Mizrachi. The ancient Jewish communities of Italy, Greece, the Caucuses, Yemen and Ethiopia form highly distinctive Jewish cultures. Converts have also formed idiosyncratic Jewish cultures, such as the various 'Black Hebrew' communities that claim descent from the ancient Israelites, but are usually not accepted as Jewish by most Jews.

▶ The vulnerability and possibility of the Diaspora

The Diaspora was both a vulnerable condition and one replete with possibilities. Jews were subject to persecution and expulsion, but they also developed transferable skills and international connections that allowed them to survive. Throughout history, other less mobile peoples have disappeared while the Jewish people have endured.

Jews have tended to settle in towns and cities, concentrating on professions that were portable. With their international contacts, Jews have always been ideally placed to profit from global trade routes. It was trade, for example, that led Jewish communities to be formed in India as far back as the Second Temple period. Jewish traders from Baghdad formed the nucleus of new Jewish communities in places as far afield as Hong Kong in the 19th century. Jews have often been most at home in cosmopolitan port cities such as Alexandria and Odessa. In medieval Western Europe, Jews were often compelled to serve as moneylenders, as usury was prohibited to Christians. The Jewish emphasis on learning meant Jews could also fill a niche as physicians.

▲ An illuminated medieval Haggadah, used in the Pesach *seder* meal.

Anti-Semitism – hostility to Jews – is a recurrent theme in Jewish history and will be discussed in more detail in Chapters 7 and 8. One of its principal effects was to uproot communities and, in so doing, disperse Jews more widely. Expulsions from England in 1290 and Spain in 1492 created new Jewish communities elsewhere in Europe and the Mediterranean. Persecution in the Russian Empire in the 19th century led to millions of Jews emigrating to the US and the British Empire. Where Jews were allowed to settle, they were often restricted to what came to be called 'ghettoes'.

The pre-modern world offered one major advantage to Jews: they were able to exercise a considerable degree of self-government. If Jews paid their taxes and stayed within the confines they were allotted, then they were often left alone. This meant that Jews remained in tightly knit communities, within which they intermarried.

Jewish communities across the world were connected through complex networks of travel and letter-writing. As a highly literate people, they shared a common lingua franca, classical Hebrew, which facilitated correspondence among educated Jews. Jewish communities would often come to the aid of their beleaguered brethren, paying ransoms for hostages, for example.

Within the Diaspora there was constant innovation in Jewish thought and practice. The Talmud was put together in the great rabbinical academies of Babylonia in the first few centuries CE. Medieval Jewish philosophers living in the Arab world, such as Saadia Gaon and Maimonides, worked to reconcile Greek philosophy with Jewish thought. Medieval Moorish-ruled Spain saw a flourishing of Jewish literature in conditions of relatively peaceful Muslim–Jewish–Christian coexistence, some-times called the 'Golden Age'. Many of the great works of the Kabbalah, the Jewish mystical tradition, were developed in medieval and early modern Spain, North

Africa and Palestine. Hassidism, the popular movement for joyful worship, swept Eastern Europe and the Russian Empire across the 18th century. Distinctive forms of Jewish music and art also developed around the world, adapting local, non-Jewish styles.

▶ The threat and promise of emancipation

From the 18th century onwards, wider changes in society transformed Diaspora Judaism, initially in Europe and the US and eventually throughout the world. In what is known as the Enlightenment, European and American thinkers mobilized the concept of reason to rethink the nature of government, the state and society. Epoch-making events in the late 18th century, such as the French and American Revolutions, spurred the development of the modern state based on citizenship and democracy.

Enlightenment thinkers did not agree on the Jews: some saw emancipation as a precondition of true enlightenment, whereas others argued that the Jews represented a primitive source of difference and must disappear completely. Jewish thinkers were themselves part of the enlightenment process. The 17th-century Dutch Jewish philosopher Baruch Spinoza was an important influence on the Enlightenment. His unconventional ideas, which denied many key Jewish tenets, resulted in his 'excommunication' in 1656 from the Amsterdam Jewish community. Later, 18th-century Jewish thinkers such as Moses Mendelssohn advocated an enlightened, rational Judaism that was fully engaged in the wider world. This movement was known as the *Haskalah*.

Enlightened thinking engendered the growth of science and scholarship in the 19th century. Modern scholarship challenged basic principles of Judaism and Jewish history. Not only did science appear to question religious faith, but modern textual criticism showed that Jewish texts were human, historically specific, creations.

As the 18th and 19th century continued, many of the restrictive conditions under which European Jews lived began to fall away in a process called emancipation. Through a series of measures begun during the French Revolution and continued under Napoleon, French Jews were declared French citizens. Napoleon spread emancipation in some of the territories he conquered, including parts of what was to become Germany. In the UK, the 19th century saw Jews gain full civil rights, and in 1858 the first Jewish MP, Lionel de Rothschild, took his seat in the House of Commons. Even in non-democratic societies, such as the Russian Empire, Jews began to enter public life in significant numbers.

But emancipation had a sting in its tale. Whereas in pre-modern societies Jews were largely left to run their own affairs, in emerging modern societies they became part of the wider world. Emancipation produced a 'crisis' of Judaism. Jews now had options that they had rarely had throughout history, including the option to not be Jewish at all. Faced with these choices, the 18th and 19th century saw the development of a host of new approaches to Judaism.

In a famous speech on 23 December 1789 to the French National Assembly, the Compte de Clermont-Tonnerre encapsulated up the double-edged sword of emancipation: 'The Jews should be denied everything as a nation, but granted everything as individuals. They must be citizens... there cannot be one nation within another nation.'

▶ Assimilation and conversion

Some Jews responded to the challenge of emancipation by abandoning their Jewishness. Given the lengthy history of anti-Semitism, it was understandable that some took the opportunity to become 'like everyone else'. A considerable number of significant figures in 19th-century Europe were either assimilated Jews or the children of converts to Christianity, among them: Benjamin Disraeli, Gustav Mahler and Felix Mendelssohn.

Anti-Semites did not let assimilated Jews or their descendants forget their origins. Assimilated Jews often retained a sharp sense of marginality that pushed them to act as critics and iconoclasts. Sigmund Freud and Karl Marx were among those whose lingering Jewishness engendered an ability to understand otherness in its various forms. The Marxist writer Isaac Deutscher coined the term 'the non-Jewish Jew' to describe those who, like himself, rejected Jewish religious practice and communal life, but whose Jewish identity continued to shape their world-view.

A less drastic step than assimilation was to be a citizen in public and a Jew in private – Judaism would be a religion only, rather than a distinctive ethnicity or nationality. This approach was embodied by the wealthy Anglo-Jewish gentry who dominated the British Jewish community until the mid-20th century. They tried to ingratiate themselves into the British Establishment and win better conditions for Jews through being model Englishmen. The synagogues they attended aped the style of Anglicanism, with clergy wearing dog collars and a Chief Rabbinate modelled on the archbishopric of Canterbury. Similar strategies could be found throughout the Diaspora as Jews sought to demonstrate their loyalty to their native countries and the compatibility between Judaism and citizenship. In the First World War, Jews volunteered for combat enthusiastically on all sides of the conflict and were encouraged by the leaders of their communities to do so.

▶ Jewish 'success'

The combination of emancipation, enlightenment and the transformation of ecomomic life offered extra-ordinary new opportunities. Jews were able to leverage certain features of Jewish society into advantages in a more meritocratic society. High levels of literacy and transnational contacts were plusses in capitalist economies. The low-status occupations that Jews had been pushed into in pre-modernity, such as moneylending and trading, now formed the basis for lucrative capitalist enterprises. One example is the Rothschild dynasty, one of the major European banking houses of the 19th century. Meyer Rothschild was born in a ghetto in Frankfurt in 1744 and from these humble beginnings became banker to a number of German rulers, before sending his children to start banks in other European countries. British and Austrian branches of the family were elevated to the nobility – the ultimate sign of acceptance into the Establishment.

Jews also played an active part in the dynamic and expanding fields of scholarship, science and the arts. For example, Austrian Jewry contributed such important figures as Arnold Schoenberg, Stefan Zweig, Arthur Schnitzler, Karl Kraus and Karl Popper.

Modernity, therefore, brought considerable Jewish 'success', materially, socially and culturally. But this success needs to be qualified. There were large sections of the Jewish world that were not touched by these developments. Eastern European, Russian and most Mizrachi were largely poor and oppressed. Further, the success and respectability of some Jews did not eradicate anti-Semitism.

Emancipation and modernity did not, therefore, 'solve' the challenges of Jewish existence. Indeed, modernity created unprecedented upheaval as Jews struggled to make sense of a new reality. In the next two chapters we will look at how different Jewish responses to modernity created deep fissures within the Jewish people.

Divisions

▶ Orthodox Judaisms

One way of responding to a time of rapid transformation was to insist that since halacha was eternal, Judaism should continue unchanged. This has come to be known as 'Orthodoxy', although not all Jews who follow this kind of Judaism like the term, preferring 'traditional', 'observant', 'Torah true' or other formulations.

Connections: A light bulb joke

Q: How many Orthodox Jews does it take to change a light bulb?

A: CHANGE????

There have been many different approaches to modernity within Orthodoxy. One response is encapsulated in the dictum of the 19th-century rabbi Moses Sofer, *Hadash asur min ha-Torah* ('Everything new is prohibited by Torah'). For a significant section of the Jewish world, the best response to modernity was to withdraw oneself as much as possible from it.

This approach lies at the heart of what is now called *Haredi* (literally 'fearful') or ultra-Orthodox Judaism. What was to become the Haredi Judaism was initially divided in the 19th century between Hassidic Jews, who emphasized mysticism and joy in prayer, and Mitnagdic Jews, who bitterly opposed Hassidism owing to their lack of commitment to Jewish study. Over time this divide has eroded, although not completely. The Haredi world is also divided into the followers of particular *rebbes* ('masters'), who are revered as teachers and authorities, even as living saints.

Connections: A light bulb joke

Q: How many Haredim does it take to change a light bulb?

A: What is a light bulb?

The Haredi world was decimated in the Holocaust and the remnants responded in the post-war period by having large families. Today Haredi families of nine or ten children are not uncommon, ensuring rapid population growth. Haredi communities are clustered in a few centres such as Bnei Berak in Israel, Stamford Hill and Gateshead in the UK, Brooklyn in the US, and Antwerp in Belgium. Haredi men study for years in *yeshivot* and usually receive minimal secular education. The emphasis on study is so great that a sizeable proportion of Haredi men do not work. State benefits, together with donations from Haredi and Orthodox philanthropists, ensure that the Haredi community can support a large non-working population.

Haredi Jews have attracted small but significant numbers of Jewish 'converts' who have assumed a Haredi lifestyle, known as *baal teshuvah* ('repentant'). One Haredi sect that has made a great effort to attract baalei teshuvah is Chabad/Lubavitch. Under the leadership of

▲ Haredi Jewish men, dressed in long black coats and hats.

Rabbi Menachem Mendel Schneerson (known as 'The Rebbe') from 1951 to 1994, the sect made a concerted effort to conduct outreach with non-observant Jews. The sect is also known for its fervent belief in the imminence of the Messianic age. Sections of Chabad/Lubavitch still believe that The Rebbe will return from the dead as the Messiah.

Connections: A light bulb joke

Q: How many Lubavitchers does it take to change a light bulb?

A: None, the old one never died.

In contrast to Haredi Judaism, 'modern Orthodoxy' emerged in the 19th century from the conviction that one could reconcile an Orthodox life with active participation in the wider society. Nineteenth-century rabbis such as Samson Raphael Hirsch, and later rabbis such as Joseph B. Soloveitchik, tried to marry halachic observance with secular work and learning. Hirsch's influential concept of *Torah im Derech Eretz* ('Torah with the way of the world') holds that Judaism can be woven into the fabric of modern life. Modern Orthodox Jews have careers and participate in contemporary culture while remaining fully committed to the observance of mitzvot.

Initially, Orthodoxy saw Zionism – the movement to found a Jewish state of Israel, discussed later in this chapter – as a blasphemous pre-empting of the messianic age when all Jews would be returned to Zion. This is still the position of a significant proportion of the Haredi world. The Neturei Karta sect has become famous for making common cause with pro-Palestinian activists. Anti-Zionism has not stopped Haredi groups from settling in Israel, although some do not vote and few serve in the army or recognize Israel's Independence Day.

Rabbi Abraham Isaac Kook (known as 'Rav Kook'), who in 1924 became the Ashkenazi Chief Rabbi of Palestine, was a key figure in reconciling a substantial section of Orthodoxy with Zionism. Religious Zionism views God's promise of the land of Israel to the Jews as inalienable and that a return to the land can be brought about by human agency. Religious Zionism has become increasingly important in Israel in the last few decades and in its more extreme forms has become highly chauvinistic.

▶ Non-Orthodox Judaism

Reform Judaism emerged in the 19th century in Germany and later spread to the UK, America and elsewhere in the Jewish world. It sometimes goes by the alternate names of 'liberal' or 'progressive' Judaism. It was conceived as a rational faith for a rational age, shorn of superstitious dogma, outdated practices and ethnic separatism. Jewish law and Jewish texts were viewed as having been created by humans, albeit (in some Reform theologies) 'divinely inspired'. Individual Jews have the freedom to decide on the practices they chose to follow. Reform synagogues use the vernacular as well as Hebrew in their worship and services tend to be characterized by decorum, avoiding the fervour of Orthodoxy.

Connections: A light bulb joke

Q: How many Reform Jews does it take to change a light bulb?

A: Anyone can change it whenever they want to.

One of the key statements of Reform Judaism was the 1885 'Pittsburgh Platform' of the American Reform movement. The platform defined Jews as a religious community, rather than a nation or ethnicity. It affirmed belief in God but sought to reorient Judaism towards 'moral' rather than 'ritual' laws. Practices such as kashrut were rejected in favour of a commitment to social justice and moral behaviour. In recent decades, Reform Judaism in America and elsewhere has begun to move away from the principles embodied in the Pittsburgh Platform. Greater value is now accorded to mitzvot, and services have incorporated greater use of Hebrew and traditional styles of worship.

Another form of non-Orthodox Judaism is Conservative Judaism. Compared to Reform Judaism, Conservative Judaism is more traditionalist. The Conservative movement grew rapidly in the first decades of the 20th century to become the largest American denomination. Theologically, Conservative Judaism includes a spectrum of beliefs: at one end are those who believe it is possible for Judaism to be consistent with halacha while finding ways round some of the more onerous restrictions; at the other end are those who share Reform Judaism's radical ideology but accord a greater value to traditional practice.

Connections: A light bulb joke

Q: How many Conservative Jews does it take to change a light bulb?

A: We'll set up a committee.

For all of the radicalism of Reform and Conservative Judaism when compared to Orthodox Judaism, they took many years to reform some aspects of Judaism. Sally Priesand, the first female US Reform rabbi, was only ordained in 1972, and the first Conservative female rabbi was ordained in 1985. Reform seminaries began ordaining gay and lesbian rabbis In the 1980s but the first openly gay Conservative rabbi in the US was ordained only in 2011. Since the 1990s, most Reform movements worldwide have gradually embraced same-sex unions and marriages but Conservative movements are divided on the issue. Reform and Conservative Judaisms long maintained other pillars of Jewish identity, such as only accepting the children of Jewish mothers as Jewish. It is only relatively recently that some Reform movements have accepted the children of Jewish fathers as Jewish.

▶ Political divisions

In pre-modern societies Jewish involvement in politics was largely confined to appointing representatives who would intercede with rulers on their behalf. In Europe these were known as *shtadlanim* ('intercessors'). Post-emancipation, Jewish communities developed institutions to represent Jewish opinion to government, such as the British Board of Deputies. Such bodies were dominated by those who had achieved prosperity and respectability in the wider society. The philanthropist Moses Montefiore, who had been ennobled by Queen Victoria, served as President of the Board of Deputies from 1835 to 1874.

The political strategy favoured by Europe's Jewish communal grandees was to emphasize the respectability of themselves and their communities. They worked quietly, eschewing public lobbying or anything that smacked of a 'Jewish vote'. This strategy often bore fruit; steady progress over the course of the 19th century in Britain saw Jews accepted into most areas of public life. While this approach did remove many of the formal impediments to Jewish participation in modern life, it didn't necessarily stop anti-Semitism. Further, it often did not satisfy the aspirations of poorer Jews.

▶ Jewish radicalism

A well-integrated and wealthy Jewish elite failed to stop the emergence of Jewish radical politics in the last decades of the 19th century. Jewish radicals saw the emancipation of Jews as an integral part of human emancipation.

There were significant numbers of Jewish Bolsheviks involved in the 1917 Russian Revolution. Although still a minority, they were prominently represented at the higher echelons of the party with figures like Trotsky and Zinoviev. In the early years of the USSR, literature and arts by Jewish authors, including Yiddish theatres and newspapers, initially flourished. However, in the 1930s under Stalin, there was an upsurge in official anti-Semitism, with most leading Jewish Bolsheviks purged, exiled or killed. In the post-war USSR, Jewish life was highly constrained and Jews who wished to emigrate to Israel were persecuted.

However, in the 1920s and 1930s at least there were good reasons for Jews outside the USSR to support communist parties. Communists were at the forefront of opposition to fascism and the hundreds of Jews who volunteered to fight in the Spanish Civil War often did so under a communist banner. The wartime Jewish Anti-Fascist Committee, formed in the USSR on Stalin's orders, helped to keep Jews in the communist camp.

There were alternatives for radical Jews suspicious of Bolshevism. The trade union movement was an important site for Jewish political activity. Jews formed the backbone of some 20th-century unions, such as the US-based International Ladies' Garment Workers' Union. Jewish union branches, would ally with other immigrant communities in striking and fighting for better working conditions.

Another important part of Jewish radical history was the General Jewish Labour Bund. Founded in 1897 as a socialist party, it sought to unite all Jewish workers in the Russian Empire. The Bund's distinctive approach to socialism was to push for recognition as a nation within the countries that Jews lived, a nation based on a shared language (Yiddish) and a distinctive secular culture. The Bund was a popular movement in Eastern Europe, rivalling Zionism and Bolshevism in popularity. Following the Russian Revolution, the Bund ceased to exist in the

Soviet Union and many Bundists were absorbed into the Soviet Communist Party. It remained an international movement with branches in Eastern Europe, the US and elsewhere. The Holocaust and the post-war triumph of Zionism meant that Bundism rapidly declined.

In the 1960s a 'New Left' emerged in Western countries which emphasized anti-imperialism and resistance to US actions in Vietnam and elsewhere. Jews were once again prominent in this movement, with radicals such as Jerry Rubin and Abby Hoffman involved in the US countercultural protests of the late 1960s and Daniel Cohn-Bendit a leader of the French student protests of 1968. Jewish intellectuals, such as Herbert Marcuse, were among the inspirations for the New Left. At the same time, the New Left's anti-imperialism led it to become critical of Israel and Zionism. This led to tension with the Jewish community and the alienation of the Zionist left.

Jewish radicalism has become less popular in recent decades due to disillusionment with communism, alienation from the anti-Zionist left and the increasing prosperity of Jews in the post-war period. That does not mean that Jews have all become conservatives. Rather, the most common position, at least in the English-speaking world, has been a centrist liberalism. Many Jews were supporters of the struggle for civil rights in the US, most famously with Rabbi Abraham Joshua Heschel marching at Selma with Martin Luther King in 1965. In the US, Jews vote overwhelmingly for the Democratic Party – in 2008, 78 per cent voted for

Barak Obama. In the UK, surveys have shown Jews to be significantly more liberal than most Britons on issues such as capital punishment and sexual morality.

Connections: Radical universalism

Radical Jews often sought to 'transcend' their origins in favour of a wider commitment to human liberation. The German Marxist leader Rosa Luxembourg declared in 1916: 'Why do you come to me with your special Jewish sorrows? I feel equally close to the wretched Indian victims of the rubber plantations in Putamayo, or to the Negroes in Africa... I cannot find a separate corner in my heart for the ghetto.'

▶ Zionism

Just as Czechs, Germans and Italians developed their own forms of nationalism in the 19th century, so did Jews. The movement for a Jewish nation state became known as Zionism. For Zionists, a Jewish state would solve the Jewish problem. Without a state of their own, Jews would always be subject to the whims of the majority. A nation state would give Jews status in the world.

Although early Zionists did consider other sites for a Jewish state, Zionism soon became focused on building a state in what was then Ottoman-ruled Palestine. The Jewish connection to *Eretz Yisrael* ('the land of Israel') had endured over the millennia of exile, not just liturgically but in a near-continuous Jewish presence. Over the centuries, small numbers of Jews had made their way to Palestine and during the 19th century this migration had increased. From the 1880s, the proto-Zionist movements Bilu and Hovevei Zion promoted Jewish settlements in Palestine, such as Rishon LeTzion, founded in 1882.

As we shall see in the next chapter, in the last decades of the 19th century anti-Semitism seemed to be worsening. Against this backdrop, many secular Jews began to lose faith in assimilation. One such Jew was the Austrian Jewish writer Theodor Herzl. In 1896 Herzl published *Der Judenstaat* ('The Jewish State') which argued that the only solution to anti-Semitism was an independent Jewish state. Herzl convened and chaired the First Zionist Congress in Basle in 1897, which agreed on a common platform known as the 'Basle Programme', which declared that:

> *Zionism seeks to establish a home for the Jewish people in Eretz-Israel secured under public law.*

Early Zionism saw Palestine as, if not a land empty of inhabitants, then certainly one where the existing Muslim and Christian Arab population were simply a subset of the wider Arab world, without national consciousness of their own. While some Zionists were more aware of the rights of the pre-existing non-Jewish Palestinian population than others, the general failure to appreciate the possibility of non-Jewish Palestinian nationalism has had long-term consequences.

Palestine was, until 1917, ruled by the Ottoman Empire. Herzl (who died in 1904) and other early Zionists negotiated with Ottoman rulers to allow Jewish settlement and also with the other colonial powers. This lobbying bore fruit in 1917, when British forces captured Palestine during the First World War. In the 'Balfour Declaration' of November 1917, the British foreign secretary Arthur Balfour told Baron Walter Rothschild and the Zionist Federation of Great Britain that:

> *His Majesty's government view with favour the establishment in Palestine of a national home for the Jewish people, and will use their best endeavours to facilitate the achievement of this object, it being clearly understood that nothing shall be done which may prejudice the civil and religious rights of existing non-Jewish communities in Palestine, or the rights and political status enjoyed by Jews in any other country.*

In Chapter 9 we will look at how Jewish settlement in Israel grew during the period of British control of Palestine, leading to the declaration of an independent state in 1948.

Zionism was based on the conviction that Diaspora Jews could never be fully free as anti-Semitism could never be totally eradicated. Jews in the Diaspora had internalized their oppression and were physically weak and submissive. Zionism would create a new man in Palestine: secular, proud and physically fit – what the Zionist leader Max Nordau called the 'Muscle Jew'. Zionism was a form of Jewish reinvention, even rebirth. Settling in Palestine became known as *aliyah* ('ascent').

In anticipation of attracting immigrants from across the Jewish world, Palestine needed a lingua franca. Hebrew was an obvious choice but it had not been a spoken language for thousands of years. In the late 19th century Hebrew was reinvented as a modern language, thanks to the efforts of a number of pioneers, most importantly Eliezer Ben-Yehuda. Ben-Yehuda systematically reformulated Hebrew, with a European-based grammar and hundreds of new words. The new language took off among the settlers in Palestine and within the wider Zionist movement.

Zionism was bitterly opposed by many sections of the Diaspora. Orthodox Jews saw it as blasphemous. Assimilated, liberal and wealthy Jews were horrified by its premise that Jews could never be truly welcome in the Diaspora. Radical Jews saw Zionism as a distraction from the universal work of liberation. But as Jewish settlement in Palestine grew, so did support for Zionism. Zionism also proved itself adept at reconciling itself with other religious and political currents. From the 1920s the Yishuv (the Jewish community in Palestine, from the Hebrew for 'settlement') was dominated by the Labour Zionist stream, which emphasized collectivism, embodied in the *kibbutz* collective farms. This meant that Zionism became more congenial to those Jews of a left-wing persuasion. Labour Zionism was opposed by the revisionist Zionism of Ze'ev Jabotinsky, that took a non-collectivist and territorially maximalist approach. The cultural Zionism of Ahad Ha'am focused on developing Israel as a global Jewish cultural centre.

▶ Conservatism

In the post-war period, the majority of Jews in the US, UK and most 'Western' countries moved up the social scale and became distanced from the working class and its politics. The 1960s New Left alienated many in its opposition to Israel. Proponents of multicultural anti-racist politics were often more concerned with post-war immigrants than Jews. Changes in sexual morality and reforms that went with it were not to the liking of many Orthodox Jews. Jews therefore became more prominent in right-wing parties.

There was a heavy Jewish involvement in the 'neoconservative' movement that emerged in the 1960s and 1970s. Jewish intellectuals such as William Kristol and John Podhoretz developed a conservatism based on strong support for Israel, an aggressive foreign policy and free market reforms. The previously liberal Jewish journal *Commentary* developed as an influential American conservative voice. The neoconservatives reached the pinnacle of their influence during the George W. Bush presidency, helping to formulate the 'war on terror' and the invasion of Iraq. Common ground has also been found between the Jewish right and Christian fundamentalists over support for Israel.

Anti-Semitism

Anti-Semitism refers to suspicion, hatred and discrimination against Jews. The term was popularized in the 1870s by a German self-defined anti-Semite Wilhelm Marr. 'Semitic' is the term used for Middle Eastern peoples who speak languages like Hebrew and Arabic. In seeing Jews as Semitic, the likes of Marr were suggesting that Jews were irredeemably foreign to European society.

Hatred of Jews is a feature of many societies but the form that it takes varies considerably. One distinction is between Jew-hatred as a subset of a wider hatred of difference and more ideological forms of anti-Semitism. In the former category we might place the pre-Christian Roman Empire. The Romans ended Jewish sovereignty in 70 CE, crushed subsequent Jewish rebellions and sold Jews into slavery, but this was the fate of many other peoples in the Roman Empire. Jews could and did become citizens in other parts of the Roman Empire.

▶ Anti-Semitism in Christianity and in Europe

A key factor in the development of anti-Semitism as an ideology was the rise of Christianity. Christianity developed out of Judaism and it was against Judaism that the first Christians defined themselves. The Jews' rejection of Jesus' divinity was compounded by what the Early Church Fathers came to see as their collective responsibility for his crucifixion. As the New Testament canon was fixed in the first few centuries CE, the debt Christianity owed to Judaism was obscured and the depiction of Jews became more unflattering. The gospel of Matthew (27: 24–5) implied that the Jews sought Jesus' death and that the Jews' words 'His blood be on us, and on our children' condemned them to a perpetual curse. By the 4th century, when St John Chrysostom wrote his *Adversus Judaeos* ('Against the Jews'), anti-Semitism had permeated the Church.

It was in the medieval period, when the Catholic Church and the centralized state grew in power, that anti-Semitism became more extreme. In many places Jews were confined to certain locations and made to wear distinctive clothing. Jews were pushed into despised but necessary occupations such as moneylending. This compounded the marginality of Jews and created a long-lasting stereotype of Jews as crooked and greedy. Jews became scapegoats in the popular imagination, as evil, mysterious and even possessing of magical powers. Jews were often accused of poisoning wells during the Black Death and, in so-called 'blood libels', were charged with the ritual murder of Christian children, drinking their blood or using it to make matza during Passover.

Blood libels were often followed by the mass slaughter of Jews. In England in 1144, the Jews of Norwich were accused of the murder of a boy called William, who was later turned into a martyr. A spate of other blood libels followed in subsequent decades, culminating in massacres in London and York in 1189 and Norwich in

1190. Times of heightened religious passion were usually bad news for Jews, as during the First Crusade in 1096 when thousands were slaughtered in Germany and France.

The attitude of Church and secular authorities to popular anti-Semitism varied. Jews were useful as moneylenders and traders and were sometimes protected for that reason. While popular anti-Semitism was useful in directing hostility away from the powerful, its uncontrollable quality was not always welcomed. Some popes, such as Gregory IX in the 13th century, spoke out against violent persecution of Jews.

Although Jews could be useful, they could also be exploited. In England, Edward I taxed the Jews to finance his wars until they could no longer pay, imprisoning and killing hundreds before expelling all Jews from the country in 1290. The Church was also implicated in persecutions. The Inquisition played a major role in rooting out secret Jews following the Spanish expulsion in 1492. Church authorities and theologians would sometimes engage Jews in public 'disputations', in which Jews were urged to convert. The disputation in Paris in 1240 was followed by the burning of the Talmud and other religious books in 1244.

Catholic–Protestant conflict from the 16th century took some attention away from the Jews. While Martin Luther's *On the Jews and Their Lies* (1543) recommended harsh penalties against the Jews, Protestant lands eventually provided a more tolerant environment. The

Dutch Republic that emerged in the late 16th century allowed Jews unprecedented freedom to participate in society. In England, the Jews were readmitted in 1655 by Oliver Cromwell, in part because his radical Protestantism saw the dispersion of the Jews as a precondition for the Second Coming.

While life for Western European Jews improved to some extent in the early modern period, Jews in Eastern Europe and Russia suffered from an upsurge in anti-Semitic violence in the same period. In the mid-17th century thousands of Jews were massacred by Russian Cossacks. In the late 18th century the partition of Poland by the Russian Empire resulted in the large Jewish population of those lands facing severe restrictions and bans from residing in the rest of Russia. Pogroms – mob violence against Jews – became a feature of Jewish life in the Russian Empire. A particularly vicious outbreak occurred following the assassination of Tsar Alexander II in 1881, with millions of Jews fleeing to the US, UK and elsewhere. The blood libel remained potent, with an accusation in Kishniev in 1903 resulting in days of rioting and at least 47 deaths.

In the post-war period there have been significant attempts by Christian leaders to reject and atone for anti-Semitism. The 1965 declaration *Nostre Aetate* ('In Our Age'), promulgated by Pope Paul VI, explicitly absolved contemporary Jews from collective responsibility for Jesus' death. A significant section of Protestantism has embraced a strongly Zionist philo-Semitism (albeit one that is often based on the hope that the return of the Jews to Israel presages the Second Coming).

▶ Muslim anti-Semitism

Muslim anti-Semitism can be found throughout history, but in the pre-modern era it was generally less systematic and virulent than anti-Semitism in the Christian world. Islam and Judaism are monotheistic, venerate Abraham as patriarch and have other areas of common practice and theology. The Qu'ran and other early Islamic texts contain conflicting statements about the Jews. While there are statements that Jews (along with Christians) are of particular closeness to God, there are also passages that appear to denounce them. Scholars and theologians, both Muslim and non-Muslim, disagree on whether these criticisms are directed at specific Jewish tribes in the Arabian peninsula during Muhammad's time, or whether they are directed at all Jews all the time.

Jews often found a more secure place for themselves in the pre-modern Islamic world than was possible in the Christian world. In some places Jews were classed as *dhimmi*, a group officially tolerated and allowed a degree of self-government, while not possessing all the rights of Muslims. At the same time, there were also sporadic persecutions and pogroms throughout Muslim history.

A more virulent anti-Semitism developed in Muslim countries from the 19th century, connected to the development of Arab nationalism against the backdrop of the rise of European imperialism. Anti-Semitism in Muslim-ruled countries was not confined to Muslims, at least at first. The 1840 'Damascus Affair', in which Jewish notables in the city were falsely imprisoned for the ritual murder of a Christian monk, was worsened by Christian–Jewish tension and resulted in a pogrom in the city's Jewish quarter. Increasing Jewish immigration to Israel in the 20th century considerably stoked tensions, and Israeli independence in 1948, and the accompanying loss of the Arab war against the new state, exacerbated the situation. Massacres were perpetrated across the Middle East throughout the 20th century and Jews were forced to leave many Muslim countries after 1948.

▶ Modern Western anti-Semitism

Post-emancipation, anti-Semitism in Europe and the 'West' both drew on and transformed Christian anti-Semitism. For the first time, Jews could be 'invisible'. Modern anti-Semitism had to be flexible enough to denounce Jews both for their separateness and for their hiddenness.

The 18th and 19th centuries saw the birth of the modern nation state, whose citizens would ideally be bound together by a common heritage, culture, language and (often) religion. Alongside the emerging concept of the nation, the rapid advancement of modern science spurred the development of particular notions of personhood and identity. A key question was why people and nations were different to each other. In 'race science', scientists postulated that humanity was divided into a number of races, with distinctive traits and destinies. The 'mixing' of races could lead only to a degeneration in 'quality'. Conveniently, 'white', 'Caucasian' or 'European' races were, it was generally agreed, particularly suited to developing advanced cultures and ruling other races.

Within this emerging racial/national paradigm, Jews were a problem. They were scattered among the nations and did not fit cleanly into any racial category. Modern anti-Semitism drew on 'scientific' research to show that Jews were literally a source of sickness; physically weak themselves, they enfeebled and endangered 'pure' nations and races. Jews were also inordinately powerful, a conspiratorial people with no loyalty to anything other than themselves. Their post-emancipation 'success' demonstrated a lust for money and power. Jews were doubly damned: if they refused to assimilate they were parasites on the nation state; if they tried to assimilate, it was only to try and take over their 'host' societies.

Two of the great causes célèbres of modern anti-Semitism reflected and intensified fears of Jewish power and subversion. The first was the conviction for treason in 1894 of the French army Captain Alfred Dreyfus. Dreyfus was convicted of passing secrets to the German ambassador in Paris. Although overwhelming evidence emerged after his trial that Dreyfus was innocent, anti-Semitism within the judiciary and the army ensured that his conviction stood. The 'Dreyfus Affair' became a huge topic of controversy in France, famously ignited by Emile Zola's 1898 pro-Dreyfus polemic, 'J'accuse'. 'Dreyfusards' and their opponents clashed not just over Dreyfus's guilt or innocence but also over the question of whether Jews could ever be loyal Frenchmen. Dreyfus was eventually exonerated in 1906, but not before battle lines had been drawn over the 'Jewish question' in France and in Europe.

Connections: Wagner and the Jews

The 19th-century composer Richard Wagner was an important influence on the development of modern anti-Semitism. His 1850 essay 'Judaism in Music' attacked the work of Jewish-born composers such as Felix Mendelssohn, arguing that their inability to ever be properly German/European meant that they could never produce music of any depth. Famously, Hitler adored Wagner's music, and in the modern state of Israel there has been a longstanding taboo on Israeli orchestras playing Wagner.

The second was the 'discovery' and publication of *The Protocols of the Elders of Zion* in Russia in 1903. The *Protocols* purported to be the records of a meeting of global Jewish 'Elders' in the late 19th century, in which they discussed their plans to dominate the world. They were widely circulated throughout the world and seen as proof of Jewish subversion and evil. Henry Ford in the

▲ The man at the eye of the storm: Aldred Dreyfus.

US circulated hundreds of thousands of copies; it was studied in schools in Hitler's Germany and continues to circulate to this day. The document was a forgery, adapted from a mid-19th-century satire attacking Napoleon III of France, and was exposed as such as early as 1921. The significance of the *Protocols* lies in the ease with which it was believed and its confirmation of the worst prejudices of anti-Semites. If one believed the *Protocols*, the only conclusion possible was that there was no accommodation possible with Jews; the historian Norman Cohen called it a 'warrant for genocide'. It was genocide that was to define anti-Semitism in the 20th century.

The Shoah and
Anti-Semitism Today

The apotheosis of modern anti-Semitism was the murder of approximately 6 million Jews by the Nazis during the Second World War. This has become known as the Holocaust (from the Greek for a burnt offering), but many Jews now prefer the Hebrew term *Shoah*, meaning 'catastrophe'.

German anti-Semitism was heightened after the traumatic loss of the First World War and the imposition of punitive reparations and territorial losses by the victorious Allies at the 1919 Treaty of Versailles. Anti-Semitism was a convenient explanation for the loss of the war – the Jews had conspired to ensure the defeat and Jews were behind the post-war Weimar Republic's collusion with Germany's enemies. Hitler emerged out of the far-right milieu that grew in the post-war chaos. Anti-Semitism was central to Hitler's view of the world, articulated in *Mein Kampf* in 1925 as well as in his public speeches, as a battle between the 'Aryan' races and 'subhumans', most importantly the Jews, but also Slavs, Roma and others.

Hitler's National Socialist Party, which grew rapidly in popularity in the 1920s and early 1930s, gathered together other extreme anti-Semites. Anti-Semitism was used as popular propaganda, as in Julius Streicher's crude tabloid *Der Stürmer*. But Nazism also attracted intellectuals, who further developed anti-Semitism into a pseudo-science that influenced even eminent philosophers such as Martin Heidegger.

Once the Nazis came to power in January 1933, official persecution and legal restriction of Jews progressed rapidly. Jews were expelled from the civil service and other professions while an official boycott of Jewish businesses tried to impoverish them. The 1935 'Nuremburg Laws' clarified who was to be counted as a Jew (see Chapter 1) and banned marriage with non-Jews. Similar laws prevented Jews from voting or holding public office. On 9–10 November 1938, a massive pogrom that came to be known as *Kristallnacht* ('night of broken glass') was unleashed, ostensibly in response to the shooting of a German embassy official in Paris by a Jew. Thousands of Jews were imprisoned in concentration camps and thousands of synagogues, Jewish business and homes were burned or ransacked. More than 100,000 Jews emigrated in the months after the pogrom, adding to the thousands who had already left, usually after having their property and money confiscated.

Connections: An ominous warning

At a speech in January 1939, Hitler made what in retrospect was an ominous warning:

'If the international Jewish financiers in and outside Europe should succeed in plunging the nations once more into a world war, then the result will not be the bolshevization of the earth, and thus the victory of Jewry, but the annihilation of the Jewish race in Europe!'

It took the outbreak of war, with the invasion of Poland on 1 September 1939, for the mass slaughter of Jews to be set in train. Once the war started, the Nazis assumed control of vast areas of Europe where millions of Jews lived and it was not possible to expel them all. While there were massacres from the start of the Polish occupation, most Jews were corralled into a limited number of ghettoes. They were horribly overcrowded (the Warsaw ghetto packed over 400,000 into 1.3 square miles) epidemics raged and a high death rate was inevitable. Jews were sent for forced labour and over time ghettoes were liquidated and consolidated as death and deportation reduced the numbers of residents. The German invasion of the Soviet Union in June 1941 heralded a new phase of systematic mass killing. As the rapid German advance proceeded, SS *Einsatzgruppen* gathered the Jews they found and massacred them, usually by shooting. At a ravine called Babi Yar near Kiev in Ukraine, more than 33,000 Jews were shot on 29–30 September 1941.

The Nazi strategy towards the Jews differed from region to region. In Western Europe and Germany most Jews were still alive by 1941, albeit facing severe persecution. In the Soviet Union they were massacred from the outset. In Poland many were used as forced labour. In some countries allied to Germany, such as Hungary, Jews initially had a limited measure of freedom. In some regions such as the Baltic States and Ukraine, the Nazis were assisted in killing Jews by local 'auxiliaries'. By 1942 a more centralized strategy had developed, sometimes known as the 'final solution to the Jewish problem'. At a meeting chaired by SS-Obergruppenführer Reinhard Heydrich in the Berlin suburb of Wannsee on 20 January 1942, a range of agencies agreed to co-operate towards deporting and concentrating all European Jews within the occupied areas of Eastern Europe, where the able-bodied would be used as slave labour and worked to death. The fate of those unable to work was to be a swiftly expedited death.

Posion gas, originally carbon monoxide and later cyanide, had been used for a number of years in the euthanasia of the mentally ill and disabled within Germany. By 1942 a method had been perfected for its use in the mass murder of Jews. Polish camps at Bełżec, Sobibor, Chełmno and Treblinka received deportees from liquidated Polish ghettoes for immediate killing. While there were hundreds of concentration camps throughout Germany and the occupied territories, only a few were used solely for extermination. Auschwitz-Birkenau in southern Poland, the largest camp, was used for both extermination in gas chambers and for slave labour. By the time of the camp's liberation in January 1945, more than a million Jews had been gassed there and hundreds of thousands had died through disease.

Approximately 6 million Jews were killed, starved or worked to death during the Shoah, out of an estimated figure of nearly 9 million pre-war Jews in the areas ruled by the Nazis. Ninety per cent of the Jewish populations of Germany, Poland and the Baltic States died. Those who survived often declined to resume their lives in their old countries, particularly since anti-Semitism continued in the post-war period (in Poland there were a number of pogroms shortly after the war), emigrating to Israel, the US and elsewhere. The Shoah, while it did not destroy the entire Jewish people, destroyed entire Jewish communities.

▲ The arrival of a trainload of Jews deported to Auschwitz.

▶ Understanding the Shoah

At post-war trials of Nazi leaders and other perpetrators of the Shoah, a common defence was that they were following orders and would have been punished had they refused. This was an inadequate explanation, as the Nazis were remarkably lenient to those who refused to take part in atrocities. Another defence was to have not known about the exterminations. Leading Nazis rarely talked publicly about the killings and even in direct orders they were often talked about in euphemisms. Bodies were cremated after gassing, mass killing sites were hidden in remote areas, and camps such as Treblinka were destroyed when no longer needed. Yet historians have shown that the fact of mass killings was widely known about, even if the details were not. Both

Nazi leaders and ordinary Germans often attempted to live their lives during and after the war so as to avoid discussion of troubling facts.

Connections: Himmler's 'Poznan Speech'

One of the few surviving open acknowledgements of the extermination of the Jews by a senior Nazi is a speech Heinrich Himmler made in Poznan to SS officers in October 1943:

'I also want to mention a very difficult subject before you here, completely openly. It should be discussed among us, and yet, nevertheless, we will never speak about it in public... I am talking about the "Jewish evacuation", the extermination of the Jewish people... Most of you will know what it means when 100 bodies lie together, when there are 500, or when there are 1,000. And to have seen this through, and – with the exception of human weaknesses – to have remained decent, has made us hard and is a page of glory never mentioned and never to be mentioned.'

Jews were not the only targets of Nazi persecution. The Roma were targeted for extermination; homosexuals, the mentally ill, the disabled, Jehovah's Witnesses and others were also killed and imprisoned in large numbers; Slavs were treated as less than human and in the Nazi vision of the future their numbers were to be drastically reduced through starvation and slave labour; Soviet prisoners of war died in their millions. What differentiates the slaughter of the Jews from that of other Nazi victims was the centrality of anti-Semitism in Nazi doctrine and the systematic way in which Jews were hunted down.

While some have argued that the Shoah was the result of a distinctly German form of anti-Semitism, subject peoples also perpetrated anti-Semitic crimes. In France, for example, the Nazis could not have deported Jews without assistance from local officials and police. Conversely, there were also significant numbers of 'righteous gentiles' who saved Jews. Oskar Schindler, immortalized in Stephen Spielberg's 1993 film *Schindler's List*, saved more than 1,000 Jews in his factories in Poland and what is now the Czech Republic. More than 8,000 Danish Jews – nearly all the Jews in the country – were saved on 1 October 1943 when the resistance organized their evacuation to neutral Sweden. More than 48,000 were saved in Bulgaria, which, despite being an ally of Germany, refused to hand over its Jews.

Questions of responsibility for the Shoah extend to the Allies. While many Jews did escape in the pre-war period and before the US entered the war, by the late 1930s many countries had set up quotas for Jewish refugees. At the July 1938 Evian conference to discuss the issue, most of the 31 countries present refused to increase their quotas or offered only token increases. In 1939 the 'Kindertransport' to the UK took in 10,000 children but did not admit their parents. Millions could have been saved if countries had opened their borders. Information about the gas chambers and earlier mass killings had filtered out through the Polish underground and other sources. Given this knowledge, it has been argued that the Allies could have intervened militarily to stop or hinder the killings.

Another sensitive issue is the responsibility of Jews themselves. The Nazis often relied on appointed Jewish councils, the *Judenräte*, to administer and police everyday life in the ghettoes, including compiling lists for deportation. In the camps, Jewish *Kapos* supervised inmates, often brutally. There were instances of negotiation with Nazis to save limited numbers of Jews from slaughter. In June 1944 Rudolf Kastner, a Hungarian Jewish leader, managed to evacuate more than 1,600 Jews from Hungary in exchange for gold, money and diamonds. In the post-war period instances of apparent collusion became highly controversial – Kastner was murdered in Israel in 1957.

Jews also resisted their fate. There were many Jewish partisan bands active in occupied Eastern Europe. In January 1943 Jewish resistance groups took over the Warsaw ghetto and managed to hold off the Germans in bitter fighting from mid-April to early May.

Connections: A Jewish joke from the Nazi era

Jews living under Nazi rule used humour as a form of resistance. Here is one example:

One Nazi sees another walking out of a rabbi's house. 'Why were you in a Jew's home?' he asks.

'I'm having the rabbi teach me Yiddish,' the first Nazi answers. 'That way I can listen when they are talking and discussing their devious plans.'

'That's very clever of you.'

'Yes,' boasts the linguist, pointing to his head. 'That's using my tochis*.'*

Tochis is Yiddish for 'ass'.

▶ Remembering the Shoah

Jews began to memorialize the Shoah from the end of the war. The diary of Anne Frank, a Dutch teenager who kept a diary while in hiding from the Germans and later died in a concentration camp, was first published in 1947. Primo Levi's *If This Be a Man*, recounting the Italian author's experiences in Auschwitz, was also published in 1947. Both books are now regarded as classics of 20th-century literature. In Israel, the Shoah was memorialized by the institution of *Yom Ha Shoah* (Shoah Memorial Day) and the opening of the Yad Vashem memorial in Jerusalem, both in 1953.

Despite these efforts to remember the Shoah, in the immediate post-war period its place within Jewish identity and Jewish community was not as central as it was subsequently to become. Survivors were often reluctant to talk as they struggled to rebuild their lives. Some historians have argued that in Israel, as well as in Zionist circles worldwide, the Shoah was at first almost, an embarrassment.

One of the turning points in Jewish responses to the Shoah, particularly in Israel, was the 1961 trial in Jerusalem of Adolf Eichmann. Eichmann had been one of the senior SS men responsible for the implementation of the Shoah. He had escaped to Argentina from where Israeli agents abducted him in 1960. His trial, which was broadcast on Israeli radio, featured Jewish survivors as witnesses. Eichmann was convicted and executed in 1962.

Since the Eichmann trial, remembering the Shoah has come to be seen as a key Jewish duty. Remembrance was made easier by the collapse of the Eastern European and Soviet communist regimes from 1989 to 1991, facilitating archival research, allowing travel to memorial sites and opening up discussion of the Shoah within those countries. Holocaust museums and memorials have opened all over the world, most prominently the US Holocaust Memorial Museum in Washington DC in 1993. Commemorations of the Shoah have not been confined to Jews. In the UK, Holocaust Memorial Day was officially instituted in 2001.

▶ Anti-Semitism after the Shoah

In the post-war period, anti-Semitism, at least in its more overt forms, gradually became unacceptable in public discourse in most Western democracies. More subtle forms of discrimination, such as the exclusion of Jews from golf clubs, were also eroded over the years. Yet anti-Semitism has never disappeared.

Neo-Nazis and other anti-Semitic groups remain active on the political fringes. One strategy they have pursued is to deny that the Shoah took place. 'Holocaust deniers' argue that there were no gas chambers; that the numbers of Jews who died were in the hundreds of thousands, not millions; that the Shoah 'myth' was concocted in order to gain support for the state of Israel and to extract post-war compensation.

In the communist bloc, anti-Semitism remained potent. Cold war opposition to Israel often led to Jews being targeted. An anti-Semitic campaign in Poland in 1968 led to Jews being removed from party positions and more than 14,000 fleeing the country. In the Soviet Union, Jews who wished to emigrate to Israel were usually refused permission to do so, becoming known as 'refuseniks'.

In the Islamic world, anti-Semitism has become closely entwined with opposition to Israel. Before and after the establishment of the state of Israel in 1948, Jewish communities in many Muslim countries faced riots and official persecution. In Iraq, for example, 200 Jews were murdered in a Baghdad pogrom in 1941, and from 1948 Jews were expelled from many professions. Today the rhetoric used in Muslim opposition to Israel is sometimes anti-Semitic. For example, the Iranian President Mahmoud Ahmadinejad has publicly denied the Holocaust on a number of occasions.

The existence of Israel has complicated questions of anti-Semitism. There is no unanimity over where criticism of Israel stops and anti-Semitism begins. Following the outbreak of the Second Intifada in 2000, the subsequent breakdown of the peace process and the global criticism of Israel that followed, it has been argued that we are witnessing the rise of a 'new anti-Semitism'. This form of anti-Semitism, it is alleged, attacks Jews under the guise of attacks on Israel. During periods of conflict in Israel, physical assaults on Jews and other forms of attack (such as vandalism) have tended to rise in the Diaspora. Critics of Israel are sometimes accused of resorting to venerable anti-Semitic tropes. For example, criticism of the power of the 'Jewish lobby' acting on behalf of Israel in the US and elsewhere can be a disguised restatement of classic anti-Semitic tropes of Jewish conspiratorial power. Further, some have argued that anti-Zionism is always anti-Semitic, given that opposition to a Jewish state denies to Jews what other peoples have.

Debates over this new anti-Semitism are exceptionally bitter, with those who are accused of it making the counter-argument that accusations of anti-Semitism are used to deflect criticism of Israel. Even among Jews there are many who argue that the new anti-Semitism does not exist or is less prevalent than its proponents claim.

▶ The effects of anti-Semitism

There is no doubt that Jewish life through the ages has been marked by anti-Semitism. But how central is it to Jewish identity? In an essay first published in 1944, Jean-Paul Sartre argued that anti-Semitism defined Jews to such an extent that Jewish identity was essentially an artefact of anti-Semitism. Some have gone further and argued that Jews have at times 'internalized' anti-Semitism as 'self-hatred', seeing oneself and one's fellow Jews as anti-Semites see them. However, the continued existence of Jewish life in countries such as the US and UK, where anti-Semitism has decreased in recent decades, suggests that anti-Semitism is not the only factor that perpetuates Judaism.

A related issue is how central a role should the commemoration of the Shoah play in contemporary Jewish life. While remembering the dead is clearly vital, an excessive focus on the Shoah can lead to a negative kind of Jewish identity. Emile Fackenheim famously argued that the '614th commandment' (traditionally, there are seen to be 613 in the Bible) was 'Thou shalt not give Hitler a posthumous victory' – that the Jewish people must survive. Yet widespread Jewish education on and consciousness of the Shoah have not prevented the decline of many Jewish communities.

The State of Israel

The foundation of the state of Israel in 1948 was a major event in Jewish history. The new state was to be a Jewish state, even if many of the Zionists who founded it were secular and ambivalent about Judaism. The attainment of Jewish national sovereignty was to propel Jews into confronting issues that had not been encountered in the Diaspora. Most importantly, Israel has forced Jews to consider questions of *power* – how to achieve it, how to wield it and how to do so justly.

▶ The formation of the state

From 1917 until 1948 Palestine was administered by the British, mandated to do so by the League of Nations, in preparation for eventual independence. Crucial to the ultimate success of Zionism was the formation of a 'state in waiting', long before independence was finally declared. The Yishuv developed its own institutions of government and worked to bring new Jewish immigrants into the country. The Zionist movement worldwide purchased land and towns and agricultural settlements were created across Palestine.

A Hebrew-speaking culture developed with remarkable rapidity. Modern Hebrew literature was created thanks to the efforts of figures such as the poet Hayim Bialik. The Hebrew University, founded in 1918 in Jerusalem, became a centre of Hebrew intellectual life. The relation of this nascent Hebrew culture to Judaism was never straightforward. While figures like Bialik drew on Jewish sources in their work and Israel attracted Jewish thinkers such as Martin Buber and Gershom Scholem to settle in the land, there was a strong emphasis on creating a new kind of Jewishness that would be totally different to Diaspora Jewishness.

Connections: Three modern Hebrew words that don't appear in the Bible

glida – ice cream

machshev – computer

musok – helicopter

The emphasis on building a new culture, as well as building settlements, helped to ensure that the Yishuv was robust enough to deal with the external challenges it faced. Faced with the rapid growth of Jewish settlement, Palestinian Arab resentment grew equally fast. The British soon found themselves having to respond to competing Palestinian and Zionist claims. Zionist–Arab–British tensions boiled over into violent conflict in the 1920s and 1930s. In response, a number of military forces developed in the Yishuv. The Haganah took a largely defensive approach and later became the core of the Israeli army. More radical underground forces such as the Irgun, Etzel and Lehi were more aggressive, attacking Arab forces and later the British, too.

British attempts to solve the deteriorating situation, either through partitioning Palestine between Jews and Arabs, or through some kind of shared sovereignty, all floundered due to Jewish and/or Arab mistrust and hostility. While the Second World War bought a partial lull in Zionist–British and Zionist–Arab tensions, caps on Jewish immigration led the Yishuv to make a concerted effort to bring in illegal immigrants. After the war, Zionist military organizations increasingly focused their operations on the British, including the use of terrorism. In 1946 the Irgun blew up the King David Hotel in Jerusalem, the headquarters of the British administration, killing 92 people.

In 1947 a United Nations commission recommended that Palestine be partitioned between a Jewish and Arab state, with Jerusalem under UN administration. The General Assembly of the UN voted to accept the plan on 29 November 1947. On 14 May 1948 the British mandate expired and the same day David Ben-Gurion, the head of the World Zionist Organization and the first prime minister of Israel, declared independence. The state of Israel was recognized by most countries, including the US, UK and USSR, but not by the surrounding Arab countries. War immediately broke out between the new state, the neighbouring Arab states and Palestinian Arab forces.

Although Israel was outnumbered in the fighting, the greater organization of the new state's forces was one factor in helping it to prevail. The war concluded with a series of armistice agreements in the first half of 1949. Israel controlled three-quarters of British mandate

▲ David Ben Gurion declaring the independence of the new state of Israel, 14 May 1948, Tel Aviv.

Palestine. The remainder of British mandate Palestine was controlled by Egypt (the Gaza Strip) and Jordan (what became known as the West Bank – the Judean and Samarian hills to the west of the river Jordan). Jerusalem was partitioned between a western Israeli side and an eastern Jordanian side, the latter including the Old City. Jerusalem became Israel's capital.

One consequence of the war of independence was the flight of around 700,000 Arab Palestinians. This has become known by as the 'Naqba' (catastrophe). Zionist historians tend to emphasize the voluntary flight of Palestinians unwilling to live under Israeli control, manipulated by their leaders' propaganda. Critics have demonstrated that Palestinians were, at least in some areas, deliberately expelled. The massacre at Deir Yassin in April 1948, in which Zionist paramilitaries massacred more than 100 residents of a village near Jerusalem, played a major part in heightening Palestinian fears.

The result of the Naqba was a Palestinian refugee problem that persists to this day. The possibility of return was made extremely difficult as Israel annexed and built on Palestinian land. Thousands of Palestinians remain in refugee camps in the West Bank, Gaza and neighbouring countries. The right to return is still a central Palestinian demand.

▶ The new state

Between 1948 and 1958 the population of Israel grew from 800,000 to 2 million as the country absorbed a wave of immigration. Some were survivors of the Shoah but more than 800,000 eventually came from Middle Eastern countries. These new immigrants, who often arrived penniless, placed considerable strain on Israel's resources and changed the previously overwhelmingly Ashkenazi demographic. The state responded with programmes of construction and job creation, particularly in the agricultural sector. Despite the challenges that mass immigration presented, Israel actively welcomed Jewish immigration and continues to do so. In 1950 a 'Law of Return' was passed that allowed all Jews to settle in Israel.

Despite Jewish immigration and the Naqba, Israel has always had a Palestinian Arab population of 15 to

20 per cent. Palestinians are citizens with equal rights to Jews: Arabic is an official language, they have the vote and there have always been Palestinian members of parliament. Most do not serve in the army, although some members of the Bedouin and Druze minorities do. However, Palestinian citizens of Israel are poorer than the general population and face significant unofficial and semi-official discrimination.

The ambivalent attitude to non-Jewish citizens of Israel is exemplified in the declaration of independence. The document declares a 'Jewish state of Israel' that 'will be open for Jewish immigration and for the Ingathering of the Exiles'. At the same time:

> ...it will ensure complete equality of social and political rights to all its inhabitants irrespective of religion, race or sex; it will guarantee freedom of religion, conscience, language, education and culture; it will safeguard the Holy Places of all religions...

Israel's national symbols are unambiguously Jewish – the flag features the shield of David and the national anthem, *HaTikvah* ('The Hope'), sings of the Jewish yearning for Zion. What it means to be a 'democratic Jewish state' has been a constant source of debate throughout Israel's history.

Israeli democracy has always been vibrant. The *Knesset*, or parliament, is elected through a particularly 'pure' form of proportional representation that ensures parties can gain seats with a smaller percentage of the vote than most other countries. Consequentially, Knessets usually feature a kaleidoscope of parties, representing many different sectors of Israeli society. Governments have always been coalitions, headed by a prime minister. Despite this, the dominant party was, from 1949 to 1977, the Workers' Party of Israel (*Mapai*) and its successor, the Labour Party. This ensured that Israel had a socialist consensus, with a largely state-controlled economy.

▶ The development of a regional superpower

A high priority for Israel was the build-up of its military. Conscription was and is compulsory, with Israeli men today serving three years, after which they are obliged to serve in the reserves for a few weeks every year; women serve at least 18 months. Heavy investment in the military ensured that the country rapidly developed a modern army, navy and air force. Israel's involvement in the 1956–57 Suez Crisis demonstrated its military prowess, overwhelming Egyptian forces in the Sinai.

Israel's most spectacular victory was in the 1967 Six Day War. Amid rising tensions with its neighbours, Israel conducted a devastating pre-emptive strike which overwhelmed Jordanian, Egyptian and Syrian forces. In six days Israel gained control of the Sinai, the Gaza Strip, Jerusalem, the West Bank and the Golan Heights. Israel was now a regional superpower, a fact only emphasized by its acquisition of nuclear weapons in the late 1960s (although Israel has never officially acknowledged their existence).

Amid great national rejoicing, Jerusalem was reunified and annexed to Israel, with the Old City and the Western Wall of the Temple now a focus for Israeli and Jewish identity. Other territories were not formally annexed, but Israel now had control over millions of Palestinians, many the descendants of those who had fled in 1948. Jews built new settlements within the occupied territories, often populated by religious Zionists who saw these territories as Jewish by right. Although the Sinai was eventually returned to Egypt in 1982 and Gaza to the Palestinians in 2005, the other territories remain under full or partial Israeli control.

Despite Israel's military might, its post-1967 wars never again achieved such startling results. A surprise attack by Egypt on Yom Kippur in 1973 resulted in a bloody war that continued for months and eventually ended in a stalemate. The invasion of Lebanon in 1982, intended to destroy Palestinian forces in the country, resulted in a long occupation before eventual withdrawal in 2000.

Post-1967, the Palestinian question came increasingly to the fore. The Palestinian Liberation Organization, under the leadership of Yasser Arafat's Fatah faction from 1969, became an increasingly independent force. From the 1970s the PLO and other Palestinian groups gained publicity for their cause with terrorist campaigns, including plane hijackings, in Israel and across the world. In 1987 the first Intifada broke out in the occupied territories, in which Palestinians demonstrated, some-times violently, against the occupation and refused to co-operate with Israeli authorities. The Intifada forced the Palestinian question onto the international agenda. At the 1991 Madrid Conference, Israel sat down to talk with Palestinian leaders for the first time.

In 1993, following secret talks in Norway, the Israeli prime minister Yitzhak Rabin and Yasser Arafat signed an agreement at the White House in the US that was to become known as the Oslo Accords. Under the agreement, a framework for resolution of the conflict was agreed in which a Palestinian Authority would initially be set up in parts of the West Bank and Gaza. The Oslo Accords were intended to lead towards a 'two-state solution', in which a Palestinian state would be set up in the occupied territories from which Israel would withdraw. Difficult issues such as the status of Jerusalem (which both sides claim as their capital) and the return of Palestinian refugees were to be resolved over time.

This two-state solution has still not been achieved. Israeli withdrawals from the territories were resisted by those who believed that they were Jewish by right and in 1995 Rabin was assassinated by a religious Jewish extremist. The Palestinians were also divided, as any two-state solution would involve renouncing claims to the entirety of Palestine. Islamic fundamentalist groups such as Hamas rose to prominence and attempted to disrupt the peace process through suicide bombings within Israel. A second Intifada broke out in September 2000 and the next five years saw more than 1,000 Israeli deaths and more than 5,000 Palestinian deaths.

Although Israel withdrew from Gaza in 2005, dismantling its settlements in the territory, there are now more

The State of Israel

than 500,000 settlers in East Jerusalem and the West Bank. Given their strong support from sections of Israeli society and the increasing militancy of some, it would be difficult to remove them. If Israel does not remove at least a substantial proportion of the settlements, then a Palestinian state that would be acceptable to most Palestinians would be hard to achieve. If Israel were to annex the territories in their entirety, it would result in a massive increase in the Palestinian population of Israel. If they were offered citizenship, then it is unlikely that Israel would remain a Jewish state. If they were not offered citizenship, Israel would cease to be democratic.

Although the principle of a two-state solution is widely shared in Israel, many of those who once supported withdrawal from the territories now feel that, were they to do so, the Palestinians would still attack Israel. The overwhelming majority of Israeli Jews are committed to the idea of Israel being a Jewish state. They reject the 'one-state solution' in which a single state would cover all of the current Israeli and Palestinian territory, partially because they fear becoming a persecuted minority in a Palestinian majority state. The one-state solution is supported by many Palestinians and is gaining ground outside of Israel–Palestine, too. Zionism is sometimes seen as a form of racism and Israel an 'apartheid' state that deserves to be boycotted economically and culturally. This is seen by Israel's defenders as 'delegitimization' and is strongly fought by both Israelis and Jewish supporters of Israel worldwide. Yet even within Israel, the 'post-Zionists' that emerged in the 1990s have started to rethinking the idea of a Jewish state, suggesting that Israel might need to become 'a state of all its citizens'.

▶ Israel today

Israel has developed into an urbanized, educated, prosperous state. The economy was liberalized from the 1980s and now has a thriving hi-tech sector. Israel has developed a robust Hebrew-speaking culture with flourishing literature, arts and music scenes. Novelists such as Amos Oz and David Grossman are highly regarded worldwide and the film industry is becoming increasingly renowned. Tel Aviv has developed into a cosmopolitan metropolis with a vibrant nightlife, including a strong gay scene.

Israel is also a deeply divided country and far from at ease with itself. From a population of fewer than a million in 1948, there are now more than 7.5 million Israelis. Tensions between Ashkenazi and Mizrachi sections of the population remain strong, even if the latter are more integrated than they once were. Israelis from the former Soviet Union, of whom more than a million arrived after 1991, some with only tenuous Jewish connections, are not always well integrated. Palestinian citizens of Israel are still marginalized. The right and left – so-called 'hawks' and 'doves' when it comes to resolving the Palestinian conflict – are bitter rivals.

Then there are tensions between religious and secular Jews. When Israel was born, the country's Jews and leaders were overwhelmingly secular. Nonetheless, Orthodox Jewish authorities were given control over registering marriages and deaths. Marriage in Israel is still only possible under religious auspices, meaning that not only mixed-faith couples have to go abroad to marry, but self-identified Jews that the Orthodox rabbinate does not recognize as Jews cannot marry in Israel. Non-Orthodox denominations have no power to marry people. The Law of Return is laxer in its definition of a Jew than Orthodoxy is, meaning that people who immigrate to Israel as Jews may not be recognized as Jews by the rabbinate. This has led to situations in which immigrants who died fighting for Israel cannot be buried with other Jews. Religious–secular tensions have also arisen over other issues such as the observance of Shabbat. Israeli business, shops and public transport have traditionally shut over Shabbat and attempts to liberalize this situation have been strongly resisted by the rabbinate.

The Haredi community is a particular source of controversy. A small minority in 1948, the Haredim have grown to around 700,000. They have resisted integration into Israeli society and many sects are strongly anti-Zionist. They have always been exempted from conscription, although a small minority serve today. Haredi parties have often held the balance of power within Israeli coalitions, allowing them to extract considerable concessions and benefits. Only a minority of Haredim work and state benefits allow them to raise large families while the men spend their lives in study. All this is a cause of much resentment among non-Haredi Israelis.

Connections: Falafel

The national dish of Israel is falafel: deep-fried ground chickpea balls, served in pitta with salad and tahini. Of course, this dish is common throughout the Middle East and long predates modern Israel. What is more uniquely Israeli is chicken schnitzel served in pitta with salad and hummus: a perfect fusion of Central European and Middle Eastern food.

▶ Israel and the Jewish world

The birth of the state of Israel had a deep impact on Jewish life across the world. Coming so soon after the Shoah, it led many Jews to feel existentially safer with a Jewish state to act as a refuge. Much of the pre-war dissensus over Zionism soon collapsed as, faced with the reality of a Jewish state, Jews of all stripes came to support it. Support for Israel grew after the 1967 Six Day War, which had been preceded by fears that Israel was in danger of being destroyed – the swift victory was widely seen as a 'miracle'.

Despite this widespread support, there were significant differences between the Diaspora and Israel. Most streams of Zionism aspired to the erosion of the Diaspora. Although *Aliyah* did result in the near-total disappearance of many Jewish communities, the majority of Jews worldwide did not move to Israel. Zionism gradually learned to live with the continued existence of the Diaspora. Diaspora communities proved useful sources of support for Israel, through political lobbying by Jewish leaders and through support for Israeli charities. Israel became a focus for education and communal activity in Diaspora communities. Zionist youth movements have proved hugely popular and educational tours of Israel are a common 'rite of passage'. Despite these close connections, most Jews outside of Israel do not speak Hebrew, at least not fluently.

Whereas in the Diaspora, religious practice remains important in the identity of even non-believing Jews, a large proportion of Israelis never go inside a synagogue. It can sometimes be difficult to find traces of Jewishness in secular Israeli culture, beyond the use of Hebrew. Certainly, the love of Israel that many Diaspora Jews demonstrate is not always reciprocated. Those Israelis who were born in the country – nicknamed *sabras* – have no memories of Jewish life outside the state of Israel. At the same time, for even secular Israelis Judaism still lingers in unexpected ways. One example is the festival of Yom Kippur, during which even largely secular cities such as Tel Aviv completely shut down.

In the Diaspora, the near-consensus over Israel and Zionism has begun to break down. Whereas Jewish opposition to Israel in the post-1967 period was largely confined to Haredim and fringe leftist groups, in recent years it has become much more significant. In the wake of the breakdown of the peace process post-2000, some Jews joined the increasingly vocal criticism of Israel, creating groups such as Jews for Justice for

▲ A satirical take on the traditional Zionist view of the Diaspora from the US cartoonist Eli Valley.

Palestinians in the UK. While members of such groups are sometimes dismissed as unconnected to the Jewish community, criticism of Israel has also come to enter the 'mainstream'. The formation of the lobby group J Street in the US in 2008 was intended to support a two-state solution amidst fears that the possibilities for peace were slipping away due in part to Israeli intransigence. Such groups represent a considerable challenge to Diaspora Jewish communities that have previously seen Israel as a source of consensus that transcends other divisions.

Israel has not unified the Jewish people. Nor has it necessarily made Jews feel safer or more secure. While the existence of a Jewish state is undoubtedly valued by most Diaspora Jews as a place of refuge, the violence that sporadically engulfs Israel means it is not necessarily a safe place to be a Jew. As this book was being completed, Israeli leaders such as Prime Minister Benjamin Netanyahu were emphasizing that, if Iran were to develop nuclear weapons, Israel and hence the Jews could be threatened with a new holocaust.

10

The Jewish People Today and Tomorrow

ALL THAT MATTERS

The writer Simon Rawidowicz once described the Jews as 'the ever dying people'. Throughout history, generations of Jews have feared that they would be the last, such was their often precarious position. In modernity, this fear has continued, but now it is not just anti-Semitism that Jews fear. The new fear is that Jews will assimilate out of existence. The post-war Jewish communities of the Western world have been marked by a strange duality: on the one hand Jews are more secure than ever, more prosperous than ever and anti-Semitism is at a lower level than ever; on the other hand Jewish leaders have become increasingly insecure about the Jewish future. Jonathan Sacks, the UK's Chief Rabbi, encapsulated this insecurity in the title of a book he published in 1994: *Will We Have Jewish Grandchildren?*

These fears are not unfounded. A US survey published in 1991 showed that more than 50 per cent of Jews were marrying non-Jews. While intermarriage isn't necessarily the end of Jewish identification and involvement, it does make it much harder to stay involved. Outside the Haredi world, Jewish institutions face a constant battle to retain the interest and commitment of successive generations of Jews. Over the last couple of decades there has been a concerted attempt to nurture 'Jewish continuity' through a process of communal renewal and education. While this process has led, in the UK and US at least, to a significant amount of innovation, there are no guarantees for the future.

The world Jewish population, currently around 13.5 million, is growing slowly, at 0.6 per cent per year. Given that the world Jewish population is estimated to have been 11 million in 1945, Jews have still not recovered from the loss of 6 million Jews in the Shoah. Many Jewish communities are in decline and not only due to emigration to Israel. The UK's Jewish population declined from an estimated 450,000 in 1945 to approximately 270,000 in 2011. Such figures become even more dramatic when one considers that the Haredi population is growing rapidly. In the UK, for example, the 20 to 40,000-strong Haredi population (numbers are disputed) is growing at the rate of at least 4 per cent a year. Take out the Haredim and many Diaspora communities appear to be shrinking. The historian Bernard Wasserstein has argued that Jews will eventually vanish from Europe, outside some pockets of Haredim.

The world Jewish population is also becoming more concentrated in a limited number of locations. Globally, the Shoah and post-war emigration to Israel left miniscule or much reduced Jewish populations in many European countries and no Jews at all in much of the Islamic world. Compared to the diversity of the Diaspora a century ago, today's Jewish world is concentrated in a few locations. Israel has the world's largest Jewish population, with about 5.75 million Jews, with the US coming second with around 5.2 million. France has the highest Jewish population in Europe, with more than 450,000, while the UK, Russia and Argentina have 200,000 to 300,000.

With this demographic decline and concentration, there has been an inevitable loss of Jewish cultural diversity. Israeli Jews of Yemeni, Ethiopian or Libyan descent may be aware of their distinctive traditions, but this distinctiveness has eroded in a cosmopolitan Jewish society. Outside of Israel, even highly committed Jews live lives similar in many respects to their non-Jewish neighbours. Yiddish, for example, is barely spoken today as an everyday language outside Haredi communities, although it is kept alive as a revived language, learned in adulthood.

Those Jewish communities that do still exist are characterized by considerable institutional vitality. Jews are indefatigable institution builders. Even in small, declining communities, one can find an array of synagogues, youth groups, schools, charities supporting Israel, community centres and cultural institutions. They are supported by strong networks of philanthropy that ensure that even poor communities have substantial buildings. In the UK one study found that in 1997 there were more than 2,000 Jewish organizations in the UK, with a combined income of more than £500 million.

Connections: An Anglo-Jewish success story

Despite the modest size of the British Jewish community, it has produced a powerful model of Jewish community education. The Limmud conference has been running since 1980 and now attracts 2,500 participants for five days every December. Featuring Jews of almost every denomination and run almost entirely by volunteers, there are hundreds of sessions every day – from Talmud study, to debates about Israel, to music performances and films. Limmud has now spread across the world and is a potent source of empowerment and learning for thousands of Jews.

▶ The continued vibrancy of Jewish society and culture

Jews are much more visible than their small numbers would suggest. The global interest in the conflict in Israel inevitably keeps Jews on the front pages. More broadly, Jews have been an object of fascination throughout modernity and even before. Both anti-Semitism and philo-Semitism (love of Jews) are predicated on the assumption that Jews are important in understanding the world today.

Jews also owe their visibility to the high profile of certain individual Jews in many of the Diaspora countries in which they reside. As we saw in Chapter 5, Jews seized the opportunities presented by modernity to enter public life. There is a long list of Jews who have become prominent in a wide range of fields. In the UK we might mention: politicians such as Benjamin Disraeli in the 19th century and John Bercow (Speaker in the House of Commons) today; academics such as Simon Schama and Isaiah Berlin; writers such as Howard Jacobson; scientists such as Robert Winston; entrepreneurs such as Alan Sugar; actors such as Maureen Lipman, Stephen Fry and Sacha Baron-Cohen. In the US there are many more: actors such as Sarah Silverman, Jerry Seinfeld and Woody Allen; politicians such as Joe Lieberman; musicians such as Paul Simon and Lou Reed; even gangsters such as Bugsy Siegel. One study suggests that Jews make up 23 per cent of Nobel Prize winners and are similarly disproportionately represented in many other lists of high achievers.

▲ British Jew Sacha Baron-Cohen in his Ali G guise.

Long lists of prominent and successful Jews are all very well, but how far is there something distinctive about Jews' engagement in modern public life? It is all too easy to fall into lazy generalizations about some kind of Jewish 'genius' and these generalizations can overlap with anti-Semitic perceptions of Jews as overly powerful.

One can point to various aspects of Jewish history that have spurred Jews onwards to success. The Jewish emphasis on education has helped to create an environment in which intellectual achievement is valued. Historically, Jews were never tied to the land and relied on commerce for a living. In modern capitalism, these restrictions became assets. The history of anti-Semitism made Jews eager to escape their marginal position once they were emancipated. More recently, the modern Jewish history of success and achievement has become something of a self-fulfilling prophecy; Jews have many high-profile role models to draw on.

In some fields, Jews also drew productively on their own marginality. In the early 20th century Jews were prominently involved in the emerging American entertainment industry. The Jewish immigrants who arrived in the US in the late 19th and early 20th century, and their children, too, were in a 'liminal' position within the wider society. They did not face the engrained anti-Semitism they faced in Eastern Europe, but nor were they yet seen as true Americans. While of higher status than black Americans, they had not yet achieved the privileged status of 'whiteness' they were to attain later in the 20th century. Eager to take advantage of the opportunities presented by the new world, they entered the rapidly expanding entertainment industry in disproportionately large numbers. Here was an emerging field in which an immigrant background was no bar to entry.

Jewish business moguls were prominent in the nascent Hollywood movie business in the early century. They sought to become more fully American by building up this new industry. In the process they often changed their names so they sounded less Jewish: Samuel Goldfish became Samuel Goldwyn, Jacob Warner became Jack Warner. Name changing was also common in the early careers of Jewish entertainers: Asa Yoelson became Al Jolson, Joseph Levitch became Jerry Lewis, Jerome Silberman became Gene Wilder. While this distancing from one's Jewish origins was in part motivated by a desire to maximize one's appeal in a white-dominated US, it does not mean that the Jewish origins of performers, producers and writers did not have an impact on their work. In part, the Jewish contribution to early Hollywood lay in demonstrating how the 'American dream' of the 'melting pot' – a term popularized by the Jewish American playwright Israel Zangwill to describe the process in which disparate immigrant groups became American – should work. The first talking picture, *The Jazz Singer* (1927), starred Al Jolson as 'Jakie Rabinowitz', a son of a cantor who runs away from home to become a jazz singer, naming himself Jack Robin. The story tells how Jack Robin is estranged and then eventually reconciled with his father, singing the Kol Nidre prayer in synagogue on his father's behalf as he lies dying, while nonetheless continuing his career as a singer. The film demonstrates that Jews and other immigrants can and should assimilate into America, while still paying some kind of respect to their origins.

As well as becoming exemplars of integration, some Jews in the US entertainment industry also explored a more ambivalent, marginal position. Jews have often acted as 'translators' of black American culture, rendering it more acceptable to the white majority. In popular music, Jews such as Al Jolson, George Gershwin and Benny Goodwin were pivotal in popularizing jazz and making it more 'respectable'. Writers and producers such as Phil Spector, Carole King, Jerome Leiber and Mike Stoller all played an important role in the growth of rock 'n' roll in the 1950s and 1960s. Jews were marginal enough to identify with black American music and culture, but they were 'white' enough to make these new sounds respectable.

While it is often difficult to identify the 'Jewishness' of the work of many of the Jews in music and cinema, in other fields it is more distinctive. Jews have played an important role in comedy in the US, with performers such as Mel Brooks, Jerry Seinfeld and Woody Allen. Jewish comedians often play with stereotypes of Jews as neurotic and prone to talk rather than action. Jewish novelists such as Philip Roth and Howard Jacobson have also explored Jewish neuroses and the complexities of Jewish identity.

Despite their ubiquity, Jews in the entertainment industry have often been coy about using explicitly Jewish themes and sources in their work. In recent decades, though, there has been a move towards a much more explicit and assertive Jewish culture. For example, the music of Yiddish-speaking Eastern European Jews, known as *klezmer*, was revived in the 1960s onwards; there is now a thriving klezmer scene worldwide. More recently, there has been talk of a 'new Jewish culture', produced by 'cool Jews', which playfully and unabashedly draws on Jewish themes in often irreverent ways. One example is the US reggae artists Matisyahu, who for much of his career was an ultra-Orthodox Jew and drew on Jewish spiritual themes in his work. In a multicultural world many Jews today are less interested in integration than in exploring their rich heritage.

Connections: Jews and comics

Jews were pivotal to the development of the US comics industry. Jerry Siegel and Joe Shuster, the creators of Superman in the late 1930s, often fought Nazis during the war. Stan Lee and Jack Kirby helped to create Marvel comics and superheroes such as Spiderman. Will Eisner pioneered comics as a form of literature, with graphic novels reflecting on Jewish experience such as *A Contract with God* (1978). Art Spiegelman's *Maus* (1986–1991), one of the most critically acclaimed graphic novels of all time, is an often harrowing reflection of his father's experiences in the Shoah.

▶ Everyday Jewish culture

Part of what makes Jews Jewish is their 'everyday' culture. Jewish life is distinctive in a myriad of small, sometimes unnoticed ways. In a famous early 1960s routine, the American Jewish comedian Lenny Bruce summed up being Jewish:

> *If you live in New York or in any other big city, you're Jewish. It doesn't matter even if you're Catholic; if you live in New York, you're Jewish. If you live in Butte, Montana, you're going to be goyish, even if you're Jewish.*

> *Kool-Aid is goyish. Evaporated milk is goyish even if the Jews invented it. Chocolate is Jewish and fudge is goyish. Fruit salad is Jewish. Lime Jello is goyish. Lime soda is very goyish.*

All Drake's Cakes are goyish. Pumpernickel is Jewish and, as you know, white bread is very goyish. Instant potatoes, goyish. Black cherry soda's very Jewish, macaroons are very Jewish.

Negroes are all Jews. Italians are all Jews. Irishmen who have rejected their religion are Jews. Mouths are very Jewish. And bosoms. Baton twirling is very goyish.

Underwear is definitely goyish. Celebrate is a goyish word. Observe is a Jewish word. Mr. and Mrs. Walsh are celebrating Christmas with Major Thomas Moreland, USAF (Ret) while Mr. and Mrs. Bromberg observed Hanukkah with Goldie and Arthur Schindler from Kiaamesha, New York.

Lenny Bruce's list of Jewish things seems arbitrary. But there is no doubt that Jewishness is often expressed through things as small as the products one buys. And there is also no doubt that doing things Jewishly is about more than traditional Jewish practice.

Food has a role here. Not only does eating play an important part in many Jewish festivals, but Jews place great importance in their own food culture. Jewish dishes, particularly Ashkenazi ones such as bagels, gefilte fish and salt beef, are strong markers of Jewish identity. Even Jews who are otherwise totally assimilated may see their Jewishness in gastronomic terms. The emphasis on food is often accompanied by a suspicion of drinking alcohol. While Jews can and do drink, in European Jewish culture at least there is not the same emphasis on drinking as their non-Jewish neighbours.

It is the small things as well as the big things that mark out Jews from non-Jews. Jews often pride themselves on being able to distinguish Jews from non-Jews in public settings. Subtle clues of appearance, dress and behaviour help to identify Jews in ways that non-Jews may miss. Many Jews take delight in 'outing' Jewish public figures and compiling lists of famous people with Jewish origins.

▶ The Jewish future

As I hope this book has shown, Judaism is a complex and multifaceted religion, Jews are a diverse people with a long and extraordinary history, and Jewish culture is dynamic and fluid. Jews and Judaism are a *big* subject: this short book has discussed genocide, the fall of empires, belief in God, the nature of the modern world. Given this 'bigness', it seems hard to imagine a world without Jews. Yet as we saw at the start of this chapter, not only are there not many Jews in the world, all the dynamism of the Jewish people has not prevented their numbers falling in many communities. Perhaps the very bigness is part of what leads some Jews away from their heritage – it is easier to live without this huge weight of history and tradition.

There are no guarantees, then, that Judaism, Jewishness and the Jewish people will survive long into the future. History suggests, though, that it would be foolhardy to bet against their survival.

This 100 Ideas section gives ways you can explore the subject in more depth. It's much more than just the usual reading list.

5 books on classic Jewish texts

1   Adele Berlin, Marc Zvi Brettler and Michael Fishbane (eds), *The Jewish Study Bible* (Oxford: Oxford University Press, 2003). Based on the Jewish Publication Society translation of the Hebrew Bible, this volume draws on a huge range of commentaries, together with modern critical essays, to provide an essential resource for those interested in delving further into the fundamental Jewish text.

2   Richard Eliott Friedman, *Who Wrote the Bible?* (London: HarperCollins, 1997). An accessible discussion of the authorship of the Hebrew Bible, placing it in the context of its time.

3   Norman Solomon (ed.), *The Talmud: A Selection* (Harmondsworth: Penguin Classics, 2009). The size and

complexity of the Talmud makes it difficult to approach. Norman Solomon's translation of a selection of Talmud texts, together with his clear commentaries and explanations, makes this a relatively approachable place to start.

4   Barry W. Holtz (ed.), *Back to the Sources: Reading the Classic Jewish Texts* (New York: Simon & Schuster, 1986). While a little out of date now, this collection is still an invaluable place to start exploring a range of 'classic' Jewish texts: the Bible, the Talmud, medieval philosophy, codes of Jewish law, the prayer book, Kabbalah and more.

5   Gershom Scholem, *Major Trends in Jewish Mysticism* (New York: Schocken Books, 1996 [first published 1941]). One of the greatest figures in 20th-century Jewish thought, Gershom Scholem was instrumental in focusing serious scholarly attention on Kabbalah, the Jewish mystical tradition. Although partially superseded by the work of more recent scholars, this book manages to be simultaneously erudite, accessible and ground-breaking.

10 books on modern Jewish theology and philosophy

6   Judith Plaskow, *Standing Again at Sinai: Judaism from a Feminist Perspective* (San Francisco: Harper & Row, 1990). An influential feminist approach to Jewish theology. Plaskow argues that ancient Jewish texts need to be radically 'rewritten' to ensure that those Jews silenced by historical patriarchy can find their place within Judaism.

7   David Hartman, *A Living Covenant: The Innovative Spirit in Traditional Judaism* (Woodstock, VT: Jewish Lights, 1997). Rabbi David Hartman is a well-respected figure at the liberal end of Orthodox Judaism. Based on his understanding of the covenant with God as a marital partnership, *A Living Covenant* makes the case for a

Judaism that is faithful to Jewish tradition, while still being able to cope with the demands of a pluralist modernity.

8 Eugene B. Borowitz, *Renewing the Covenant: A Theology for the Postmodern Jew* (Philadelphia, PA: Jewish Publication Society, 1998). A major theological statement from a leading figure in contemporary Reform Jewish theology.

9 Joseph B. Soloveitchik, *Halakhic Man* (Philadelphia, PA: Jewish Publication Society, 1994). Rabbi Joseph Soloveitchik was a major figure in 20th-century modern Orthodoxy. *Halakhic Man* places halachic observance at the centre of Jewish theology.

10 Abraham Joshua Heschel, *The Sabbath* (New York: Farrar Straus Giroux, 2005). A popular work by one of 20th-century American Jewry's most prominent rabbis, *The Sabbath* argues that Shabbat is, for Jews, a 'cathedral in time', a period of heightened connection between God and Israel.

11 Dan Frank, Oliver Leaman and Charles Manekin (eds), *The Jewish Philosophy Reader* (London: Routledge, 2000). There is a centuries-old tradition of Jewish philosophy – a tradition that, sadly, this book has not had the space to cover. *The Jewish Philosophy Reader* offers readings and introductions to Jewish philosophers throughout the ages.

12 Martin Buber, *I and Thou* (Eastford, CT: Martino Publishing, 2010 [first published in German in 1923]). Part philosophy, part theology, Martin Buber's famous book offers a profound meditation on the relationship between man and man, and man and God.

13 Mordecai Kaplan, *Judaism as a Civilization: Toward a Reconstruction of American-Jewish Life* (Philadelphia, PA: Jewish Publication Society, 1994 [first published in 1934]). A rabbi and founder of the Reconstructionist movement, Kaplan argues in *Judaism as a Civilization* that

Judaism should be seen as a civilization, one that can be reconstructed to fit better into modernity.

14 and 15 Seán Hand, *Emmanuel Levinas* **(London: Routledge, 2008) and Norbert M. Samuelson,** *A User's Guide to Franz Rosenzweig's Star of Redemption* **(London: Routledge, 2010).** Emmanuel Levinas and Franz Rosenzweig were two of the most original and influential 20th-century Jewish philosophers. Their work is notoriously difficult, so it's best to begin with secondary literature or introductory guides such as the two above.

5 books on Jewish practice

16 Arnold Eisenberg, *Jewish Traditions* **(New York: Jewish Theological Society, 2008).** A comprehensive reference work on all aspects of Jewish ritual and observance, it also explains how practice differs between denominations and traditions.

17 Hayim Halevy Donin, *To Be a Jew: Guide to Jewish Observance in Contemporary Life* **(London: HarperCollins, 1998).** A no-nonsense guide to Jewish practice from an Orthodox standpoint. Its prescriptiveness might make it intimidating to some, but it provides a powerful demonstration of the complexity and detail inherent in Orthodox practice.

18 Lawrence A. Hoffman, *The Way into Jewish Prayer* **(Woodstock, VT: Jewish Lights, 2004).** An accessible guide to Jewish prayer, the book explains how it has evolved over time and what prayer means today.

19 *The Artscroll Siddur* **(various editions).** The publishing house Artscroll has become renowned for its accessibly translated, informatively annotated and clearly laid-out *siddurim* (prayer books). Although frequently used across the Orthodox Jewish world, *The Artscroll Siddur* reflects practice and theology on the Haredi-influenced right of Orthodoxy.

20 *Mishkan Tefillah – A Reform Siddur* **(various editions; first published 2007).** The most recent *siddur* produced by the American Reform movement. Beautifully produced, its use of gender-inclusive language reflects contemporary trends in progressive Judaism.

10 books on Jewish history and the Diaspora

21 **Bernard Lewis,** *The Jews of Islam* **(Princeton: Princeton University Press, 1987).** A readable, but balanced and careful, survey of the relationship between Jews and Islam, both in history and in Islamic texts.

22 **Paul Kriwaczek,** *Yiddish Civilisation: The Rise and Fall of a Forgotten Nation* **(London: Weidenfeld & Nicolson, 2005).** A history of Ashkenazi Jewry and its development into a Yiddish-speaking 'civilization'.

23 **T**he Life of Glückel of Hameln **(Philadelphia, PA: Jewish Publication Society, 2006).** These memoirs of a 16th-century German Jewish woman, offer a remarkable window into a now-vanished world.

24 **Peter Cole (ed.),** *The Dream of the Poem: Hebrew Poetry from Muslim and Christian Spain, 950–1492* **(Princeton: Princeton University Press, 2007).** An anthology of poetry from the 'golden age' of pre-expulsion Spanish Jewry. Simultaneously religious and secular, influenced by Christianity and Islam, Judeo-Spanish poetry was one of the crowning cultural achievements of the medieval Jewish world.

25 **Yirmiyahu Yovel,** *The Other Within: The Marranos – plit Identity and Emerging Modernity* **(Princeton: Princeton**

University Press, 2009). The Marranos were Jews who were forcibly converted in Spain and Portugal yet retained secret elements of Jewish identity and practice. In this scholarly work, Yovel unpicks the complex and ambivalent identities of these Jews and their descendants.

26 Paul Johnson, *A History of the Jews* (London: Orion, 2001). A complete 4,000-year history of the Jewish people by a unapologetically philo-Semitic author.

27 Paul Mendes-Flohr and Jehuda Reinharz (eds), *The Jew in the Modern World: A Documentary History* (Oxford: Oxford University Press, 1995). A comprehensive collection of extracts from books and other documents that tell the story of the Jewish people in modernity.

28 Jacob Katz, *Tradition and Crisis: Jewish Society at the End of the Middle Ages* (Syracuse, NY: Syracuse University Press, 2000 [first published 1961]). A widely influential study of the Jews on the cusp of the transition to modernity.

29 Geoffrey Alderman, *Modern British Jewry* (Oxford: Clarendon Press, 1998). The standard work on the history of the Jews in Britain since readmission in the 17th century.

30 Amos Elon, *The Pity of it All: A Portrait of Jews in Germany, 1743–1933* (Harmondsworth: Penguin, 2002). Chronicles the hopes and fears that accompanied the German Jews' transition to modernity.

5 books on anti-Semitism and the Shoah

31 Anthony Julius, *Trials of the Diaspora: A History of Anti-Semitism in England* (Oxford: Oxford University Press, 2010). A lengthy but readable work that covers the history of English anti-Semitism from medieval times through to contemporary 'anti-Zionist anti-Semitism'.

32 Ruth Harris, *The Man on Devil's Island: Alfred Dreyfus and the Affair that Divided France* (Harmondsworth: Penguin, 2011). A gripping account of the Dreyfus affair and its pivotal importance on French politics.

33 Deborah Dwork and Robert J. van Pelt, *The Holocaust: A History* (London: John Murray, 2002). Insofar as any work can grasp the magnitude of the Shoah, this book does it.

34 Peter Novick, *The Holocaust and Collective Memory* (London: Bloomsbury Publishing, 1999). A revealing study of the changing place of the Shoah in American and Jewish life. Novick is critical of what he argues is the use of victimhood as a claim for Jewish political entitlement.

35 Art Spiegelman, *The Complete Maus* (Harmondsworth: Penguin, 2003). A graphic novel that tells the story of the author's father's experiences in the Shoah and its impact on him and his son after the war. Told as a kind of masquerade – with Jews drawn as mice and gentiles as pigs – the work is both disturbing and moving.

5 books on Israel and Zionism

36 David J. Goldberg, *To the Promised Land: A History of Zionist Thought* (London: Faber and Faber, 2009). A sometimes critical but sympathetic account of Zionism as an intellectual movement and the driving force behind modern Israel.

37 Benny Morris, *Righteous Victims: A History of the Zionist–Arab Conflict, 1881–1999* (New York: Random House, 2001). Benny Morris was one of the 'new historians' who transformed the historiography of modern Israel in the 1980s and 1990s, challenging received Zionist ideas of how the state was created. *Righteous Victims* is a highly readable account of the Israel–Arab/Palestinian conflict that, while it questions elements of the Zionist narrative, upholds the validity of the Zionist ideal.

38 Amos Oz, *A Tale of Love and Darkness* (New York: Vintage, 2005). Amos Oz is Israel's most acclaimed novelist. Against the backdrop of the early years of the state, his memoir, *A Tale of Love and Darkness*, tells the story of his childhood and his parents' struggles to adapt to the new country.

39 and 40 Efraim Karsh, *Palestine Betrayed* (New Haven, CT: Yale University Press, 2007) and Ilan Pappe, *The Ethnic Cleansing of Palestine* (London: Oneworld Publications, 2007). The flight of the Palestinians from Israel in 1948 and the attitude of pre- and post-state Zionists towards them is a topic fraught with controversy. Given the lack of consensus, I have chosen two works that offer diametrically opposed views on the subject – Karsh is critical of the Palestinians; Pappe is critical of the Israelis. Both have been attacked by other scholars but both offer important insights into an intractable issue.

5 books on contemporary Jewish life

41 Samuel C. Heilman, *Defenders of the Faith: Inside Ultra-Orthodox Jewry*, 2nd edn (Berkeley, CA: University of California Press, 2000). An eye-opening ethnography of the Haredi Jewish world.

42 Keith Kahn-Harris and Ben Gidley, *Turbulent Times: The British Jewish Community Today* (London: Continuum, 2010). The first sociological study of the contemporary British Jewish community, *Turbulent Times* discusses how the community adapted to a multicultural Britain during the 1990s and 2000s.

43 Steven M. Cohen and Arnold M. Eisen, *The Jew Within: Self, Family and Community in America* (Bloomington: University of Indiana Press, 2000). A rigorous sociological study of the Jewish identity of 'moderately affiliated' Jews in America. Cohen and Eisen's book has been influential in policymaking within the US Jewish community.

44 Samuel C. Heilman, *Synagogue Life: A Study in Symbolic Interaction* (Piscataway, NY: Transaction Publishers, 1998 [first published in 1976]). Although a little old now, Samuel Heilman's sociological study of the synagogue and its place in Jewish communities remains an insightful account of an important Jewish institution.

45 Samuel G. Freedman, *Jew vs. Jew* (New York: Simon & Schuster, 2000). A journalistic account of the schisms that divide American Jews from each other.

5 books on Jewish culture

46 Michael Billig, *Rock 'n' Roll Jews* (London: Five Leaves Publications, 2000). A readable study of the Jewish contribution to 20th-century popular music.

47 Mark Slobin, *Fiddler on the Move: Exploring the Klezmer World* (Oxford: Oxford University Press, 2000). An ethnographic account of the large and expanding global klezmer music scene.

48 Neal Gabler, *An Empire of Their Own: How the Jews Invented Hollywood* (New York: Random House, 1998). An accessible history of Jews in early Hollywood, showing the pivotal contribution of Jewish moguls.

49 Michael Rogin, *Blackface, White Noise: Jewish Immigrants in the Melting Pot* (Berkeley, CA: University of California Press, 1996). A cultural history of Jews' relationship to blackness within early 20th-century popular culture.

50 Ruth Ellen Gruber, *Virtually Jewish: Reinventing Jewish Culture in Europe* (Berkeley, CA: University of California Press, 2002). There has been a heightened interest in Jewish culture in Europe in the last couple of decades. Ruth Ellen Gruber's book examines this phenomenon in detail and explains why it has happened.

5 Jewish novels

51 Howard Jacobson, *The Finkler Question* (London: Bloomsbury, 2010). Winner of the Man Booker Prize in 2010. Howard Jacobson is a British Jew who has made Jews the subject of many of his novels. *The Finkler Question* dwells on the angst-ridden nature of modern British Jewry, incorporating a scathing satire of secular Jewish critics of Israel.

52 Chaim Potok, *The Chosen* (Harmondsworth: Penguin, 2010 [first published in 1967]). Set in Brooklyn in the 1940s, *The Chosen* tells the story of the friendship between a Haredi and a secular Jewish young man against the backdrop of epoch-making events in the Jewish world.

53 Sholem Aleichem, *Tevye the Dairyman and Motl the Cantor's Son* (Harmondsworth: Penguin, 2009 [first published in 1894]). Sholem Aleichem was a Russian Jewish author who wrote in Yiddish. His stories of Tevye later became the basis for the film *Fiddler on the Roof*.

54 Naomi Alderman, *Disobedience* (London: Viking, 2006). *Disobedience* won the 2006 Orange Award for New Writers and tells the story of an Orthodox rabbi's daughter in north London grappling with her lesbian sexuality.

55 Shalom Auslander, *Foreskin's Lament* (London: Picador, 2008). A cathartic and comic attack on the orthodox world in which Auslander was raised and from which he fled.

5 Jewish publications

56 Jewish Chronicle (www.thejc.com). Founded in 1841, the *Jewish Chronicle*, a weekly newspaper, is an Anglo-Jewish institution. Although often criticized, particularly at the moment, for its perceived right-wing bias, it remains an essential source of news for the British Jewish community.

57 The Forward (www.forward.com). Founded in America 1897 as a Yiddish-language socialist daily, *The Forward* has evolved into a respected English-language weekly newspaper, while still publishing a Yiddish supplement.

58 Haaretz (www.haaretz.com). An Israeli newspaper, from a liberal-left perspective, founded in 1918. The English-language version provides an indispensable source of news and comment on Israel and the Jewish world.

59 Jewschool (www.jewschool.com). A lively, politically progressive, US Jewish blog.

60 Failed Messiah (www.failedmessiah.com). An often controversial blog that covers Orthodox Judaism, *Failed Messiah* has exposed a number of scandals within the Orthodox world.

5 Jewish-themed films (that aren't *Fiddler on the Roof* or *Schindler's List*)

61 *The Jazz Singer* (1927). The first proper 'talkie' movie, starring Al Jolson, offers a fascinating insight into early 20th-century Jewish American identity and assimilation. The 1980 remake starring Neil Diamond is less essential.

62 *Ushpizin* (2005). Israeli films have improved dramatically in the last couple of decades. *Ushpizin* is a touching story of an impoverished, childless, Haredi couple whose world is turned upside down over the holiday of Sukkot, when a pair of criminals from the husband's non-religious past turn up.

63 *The Prince of Egypt* **(1998).** A blockbuster animated version of the story of the Exodus. Jewish scholars were consulted in the making of the film, resulting in an unusually accurate depiction (for a cartoon) of an ancient Jewish story.

64 *Keeping the Faith* **(2000).** Not a classic by any means, this light-hearted tale of a rabbi (played by Ben Stiller) and a priest, and their relationship with a woman from their childhood, is still a lot of fun.

65 *Fateless* **(2005).** Based on Hungarian writer Imre Kertész's book of the same name, a semi-autobiographical account of his experiences in Auschwitz, *Fateless* shows the sheer hellishness of the experience of those who went through the concentration camps.

5 Jewish songs

At the time of writing, the originals or versions of these songs can be found on YouTube:

66 **'Kol Nidre'.** The solemn Ashkenazi tune for the opening prayer of the evening service on Yom Kippur has been adapted by many musicians. The version for cello and orchestra by Max Bruch is particularly affecting.

67 **'Am Yisrael Chai' ('The people of Israel lives'), version by Shlomo Carlebach.** Shlomo Carlebach was a US rabbi and singer whose work fused Hassidic and hippy spirituality. His 1960s setting of the biblical words of 'Am Yisrael Chai' has become popular throughout the Jewish world, although it is particularly associated with right-wing religious Zionism.

68 **'Not by Might' by Debbie Friedman.** Debbie Friedman, who died in 2011, was an American Jewish singer-songwriter, many of whose compositions and settings for prayers have been incorporated in the liturgy of Reform and other synagogues. Her song 'Not by Might' (based on Zechariah 4: 6) is one example of her English-language work.

69 **'Mehadrin Rhyming' by Y-Love.** Y-Love is a black American convert to Judaism who produces some of the most exciting Jewish hip hop today. Initially Haredi his time in a yeshiva gave him the knowledge to rap in Hebrew, Aramaic and Yiddish as well as English. 'Mehadrin Rhyming' is one demonstration of his extraordinary talent.

70 **'Sapari' by Orphaned Land.** Orphaned Land is an Israeli heavy-metal band which includes Mizrachi Jewish musical and lyrical influences in its work. 'Sapari' is based on a 17th-century Yemenite Jewish poem.

5 unusual Jewish communities

71 **Finland.** Finland, whose Jewish population is now around 1,500, is the only place where Jews fought alongside the Nazis. During the Second World War, Finland managed to remain independent while allied to the Germans. They fought for their independence against the Soviets while only eight Jews were handed over to the Nazis.

72 **Curaçao.** Curaçao, in the Dutch Antilles has the oldest active Jewish community in the Americas, dating to 1651. The community is of mostly Sephardi ancestry and today numbers around 300.

73 **Shanghai.** The international enclave in Shanghai became a place of refuges for around 18,000 Jews fleeing Europe during the Nazi period. Although virtually all left after the

Second World War, there is today a community of 2,000 to 3,000, mostly made up of Western Jewish expatriates.

74 **Lemba**. The Lemba are an African people, most of whom live in South Africa and Zimbabwe. Their oral traditions claim descent from the Jewish people and some practise Jewish rituals today, sometimes incorporated into Christianity or Islam. Genetic tests suggest that they may well be able to trace their ancestors back to biblical Israel.

75 **Iran**. The Iranian Jewish community dates back to antiquity and has deep roots in the country. Despite strong official opposition to Israel and Zionism and the use of anti-Semitic rhetoric by some Iranian leaders, 25,000 Jews remain in Iran – more than in any other Islamic country. They are equal to Muslims in the Iranian constitution and elect a member of parliament. They do, however, keep a very low profile and are obliged to distance themselves from Israel and Zionism.

5 cult figures and objects in Anglo-Jewry

76 **Mrs Elswood**. Mrs Elswood pickles are a fixture on the dinner tables of many British Jewish households. Generations of British Jews have wondered whether the smiling illustration of Mrs Elswood is based on a real person – and, more importantly, is she Jewish?

77 **Palwin.** A sickly-sweet red wine used for Jewish rituals such as Shabbat. 'Palwin' originally stood for 'Palestinian Wine and Trading Company' and is produced in Israel. It comes in the indistinguishably different flavours 'Number 4' and 'Number 10' – the numbers of the bus routes outside the London office of Palwin.

78 **Harvey Bratt**. Harvey Bratt works for the Anglo-Jewish charity the United Jewish Israel Appeal and, before that, for the Jewish National Fund. His job is to get his charity into people's wills and his face appears virtually every week in adverts in the *Jewish Chronicle* suggesting that he assist Jews of a certain age with planning their legacies.

79 **Carmelli's**. A kosher bakery in the heavily Jewish London neighbourhood of Golders Green. It opens till late on a Saturday night after Shabbat and is the inevitable destination at the end of many Jewish young people's nights out.

80 **Sacha Baron-Cohen**. Now world-famous, almost everyone in Anglo-Jewry either claims to have known Sacha Baron-Cohen before he was famous or claims to know someone who did. Given that he went to a school with a large Jewish population and was heavily involved in a Jewish youth movement, this isn't that surprising. I'm no exception: I was briefly friends with Sacha when I was eight years old.

5 Yiddish slang words that English-speaking Jews use

Most non-Haredi Jews today do not speak Yiddish, but Jews still often use Yiddish words and phrases in their conversations, including:

81 *Broigus.* A grudge or conflict.

82 *Macher.* A doer, big-shot or important person.

83 *Chutzpah.* Nerve, guts or daring.

84 *Shmuck.* A fool or idiot.

85 *Shiksha.* A derogatory term for a non-Jewish woman.

Maimonides' Thirteen Articles of Faith

The Thirteen Articles of Faith written by the 12th-century rabbi Moshe Ben Maimon, known as Maimonides, appear in his commentary on the Mishneh (Tractate Sanhedrin, Chapter 10). Although controversial at the time, a more poetic version eventually entered the liturgy at the end of daily morning prayers:

I believe with perfect faith that the Creator, blessed be His name, is the Creator and Guide of everything that has been created, and that He alone has made, does make, and will make all things.

I believe with perfect faith that the Creator, blessed be His name, is One, and that there is no oneness like His in any way; and that He alone is our G-d, who was, is, and ever will be.

I believe with perfect faith that the Creator, blessed be His name, is not a physical body, and no physical phenomena can apply to Him, and that He has no form whatsoever.

I believe with perfect faith that the Creator, blessed be His name, is the first and is the last.

I believe with perfect faith that the Creator, blessed be His name, is the only one to whom it is proper to pray, and that it is not proper to pray to anyone else.

I believe with perfect faith that all the words of the prophets are true.

I believe with perfect faith that the prophecy of Moses our teacher, peace be to him, was true, and that he was the father of all the prophets, both of those who preceded him and of those who followed him.

I believe with perfect faith that the entire Torah which we now possess is the same that was given to Moses our teacher, peace be to him.

I believe with perfect faith that this Torah will not be changed, nor will there be any other Torah from the Creator, blessed be His name.

I believe with perfect faith that the Creator, blessed be His name, knows all the actions and thoughts of human beings, as it is said, It is He who fashions the hearts of them all, who discerns all their actions. (Psalms 33: 15)

I believe with perfect faith that the Creator, blessed be His name, rewards those who keep His commandments, and punishes those who transgress His commandments.

I believe with perfect faith in the coming of the Messiah, and, though he tarry, I wait daily for his coming.

I believe with perfect faith that there will be a resurrection of the dead at the time when it will please the Creator, blessed be His name and exalted be His mention for ever and ever.

1 extraordinary passage from the Talmud

99 Said Rabbi Yochanan, 'Rabbi Ishmael the son of Yose's member was like a wineskin of nine *kav*; Rabbi Elazar the son of Rabbi Shimon's member was like a wineskin of seven *kav*.' Rav Papa said, 'Rabbi Yochanan's member was like a wineskin of three *kav*.' And there are those who say: like a wineskin of five kav. Rav Papa himself had a member which was like the baskets of Hipparenum.

This passage was translated by the Talmud scholar Daniel Boyarin in his book *Carnal Israel*. As Boyarin himself points out, not all scholars agree that the Aramaic word *evreh* should be translated as 'member', meaning 'penis'. However, whichever way you read it, the passage is a testimony to an interest in the body and its excesses within the Talmud. Boyarin's book provides a fascinating insight into this most unexpected side of this foundational Jewish text.

1 great quote about Judaism that I couldn't find a source for

100 'It doesn't matter what kind of Jew you are, provided you are ashamed of it.'

This quote is apparently from a prominent contemporary rabbi, but I have been unable to find which one. It doesn't literally imply that Jews should be ashamed of being Jewish. Rather, it suggests that whatever level of observance a Jew practises is never enough. Judaism is a journey, predicated on the inevitably flawed nature of Jews and the world. This seems an appropriate way to finish this book: the picture of Judaism I have tried to paint in this book is incomplete; it's up to you to fill in the missing bits – and whether you are Jewish or not, this task will never be complete.

Notes

Chapter 1

'There are estimated to be around 13.5 million Jews in the world today': 'Number of Jews in the world with emphasis on the United States and Israel', The Jewish People Policy Institute, 2011, online at http://jppi. org.il/uploads/Number_of_Jews_in_the_world_with_emphasis_on_ the_United_States_and_Israel_EN.pdf

Chapter 2

'Take me as a proselyte, but on condition that you teach me entire Torah...': Torah, which refers literally to the first five books of the Bible, is used here in its more general sense of Jewish teaching.

'Once, a certain gentile ...' quote: Tractate Shabbat 31a. I have adapted this translation from: Hayim Nahman Bialik and Yehoshua Hana Ravnitzky (eds), *The Book of Legends*, trans. William G. Bruade (New York: Schocken Books, 1992), p. 205.

'Let us start with Judaism as described in the Hebrew Bible': That is, the Old Testament (Jews do not recognize the Christian New Testament, written in Greek, as part of its canon).

'The Hebrew letters YHVH': This is the origin of the names 'Yahweh' and 'Jehovah' ('j' being interchangeable with 'y' in some languages). However, these are of Christian origin and are rarely used by Jews.

'the people of the book': The term originates in the Qur'an to describe non-Islamic monotheistic faiths with a revealed scripture, including the Jews, but it has stuck most strongly to Jews.

'Tanakh': A Hebrew acronym of Torah, Neviim and Ketuvim.

Story from the Babylonian Talmud: Baba Mezia 59a–59b. I have adapted this translation from: Hayim and Ravnitzky (eds), *The Book of Legends*, p. 223.

Chapter 3

'In contrast, as the theologian Abraham Joshua Heschel argued, since the destruction of the Second Temple Jews have found holiness in *time*': Abraham Joshua Heschel, *The Sabbath* (Farrar Straus Giroux, 2005 [originally published 1951]).

'The main festivals...': Some festivals are celebrated for an extra day by Jews outside Israel, originally to ensure that no mistakes were made in fixing the date.

Chapter 4

Take an average "moderately engaged" British Jew': Steven M. Cohen and Keith Kahn-Harris, *Beyond Belonging: The Jewish Identities of Moderately Engaged British Jews* (London: UJIA / Profile Books, 2004).

Chapter 5

'Writers such as Shlomo Sand have argued that the extent of post-exilic Jewish proselytization has been underestimated to the extent that it is problematic to talk of the historical continuity Jewish people': Shlomo Sand, *The Invention of the Jewish People* (London: Verso, 2009).

'On the other hand, modern genetic studies do suggest a degree of common descent for much of the Jewish people, with *Cohanim* (Jews who claim descent from the Temple priesthood) showing strong signs of a common origin': This is a complex area of scientific enquiry. David B. Goldstein's *Jacob's Legacy: A Genetic View of Jewish History* (Yale University Press, 2009) provides an accessible introduction. The 'Genetic studies on Jews' Wikipedia page has a useful collection of links.

'Enlightenment thinkers did not agree on the Jews: some saw emancipation as a precondition of true enlightenment, whereas others argued that the Jews represented a primitive source of difference and must disappear completely': See Adam Sutcliffe, *Judaism and Enlightenment* (Cambridge: Cambridge University Press, 2005).

Compte de Clermont-Tonnerre quote: cited in Paul Mendes-Flohr and Jehuda Reinharz (eds), *The Jew in the Modern World: A Documentary History* (Oxford: Oxford University Press, 1995), p. 115.

'The Marxist writer Isaac Deutscher coined the term "the non-Jewish Jew" to describe those who, like himself, rejected Jewish religious practice and communal life, but whose Jewish identity continued to shape their world-view': Isaac Deutscher, *The Non-Jewish Jew and Other Essays* (Cambridge: Cambridge University Press, 1968).

Chapter 6

'Non-Orthodox Judaism': Owing to constraints of space, this section will only discuss the Reform and Conservative movements. There are also other related movements such as Reconstructionalism and Jewish Renewal.

'One of the key statements of Reform Judaism was the 1885 "Pittsburgh Platform" of the American Reform movement': This can be viewed online at http://www.jewishvirtuallibrary.org/jsource/Judaism/pittsburgh_program.html or in Paul Mendes-Flohr and Jehuda Reinharz (eds), *The Jew in the Modern World: A Documentary History* (Oxford University Press, 1995), pp. 468–9.

'Another form of non-Orthodox Judaism is Conservative Judaism': Known as the Masorti movement in some countries.

'In the US, Jews vote overwhelmingly for the Democratic Party – in 2008, 78 per cent voted for Barak Obama': 'Jewish Vote for Obama Exceeds all Expectations', 5 Nov. 2008, online at http://www.njdc.org/site/page/jewish_vote_for_obama_exceeds_all_expectations

'In the UK, surveys have shown Jews to be significantly more liberal than most Britons on issues such as capital punishment and sexual morality': Stephen Miller, Marlena Schmool and Anthony Lerman, *Social and Political Attitudes of British Jews: Some Key Findings of the JPR Survey* (London: Institute for Jewish Policy Research, 1996).

'Why do you come to me with your special Jewish sorrows? I feel equally close to the wretched Indian victims of the rubber plantations in Putamayo, or to the Negroes in Africa... I cannot find a separate corner in my heart for the ghetto': Paul Mendes-Flohr and Jehuda Reinharz (eds), *The Jew in the Modern World: A Documentary History* (Oxford: Oxford University Press, 1995), pp. 261–2.

'Zionism seeks to establish a home for the Jewish people in Eretz-Israel secured under public law': Paul Mendes-Flohr and Jehuda

Reinharz (eds), *The Jewish in the Modern World: A Documentary History* (Oxford: Oxford University Press, 1995), p. 540.

'His Majesty's government ... other country' quote: Paul Mendes-Flohr and Jehuda Reinharz (eds), *The Jewish in the Modern World: A Documentary History* (Oxford: Oxford University Press, 1995), p. 582.

Chapter 7

'the historian Norman Cohen called it a "warrant for genocide"': Norman Cohn, *Warrant for Genocide: The Myth of the Jewish World Conspiracy and the Protocols of the Elders of Zion*, 2nd edn (London: Serif, 2005).

Chapter 8

'But Nazism also attracted intellectuals, who further developed anti-Semitism into a pseudo-science that influenced even eminent philosophers such as Martin Heidegger': Richard Wolin, *The Heidegger Controversy* (Cambridge, MA: The MIT Press, 1993).

Hitler quote – 'If the international Jewish financiers ... the Jewish race in Europe!': http://www.jewishvirtuallibrary.org/jsource/Holocaust/nazi_statements.html

'Yet historians have shown that the fact of mass killings was widely known about, even if the extent and the details were not': See, for example: Robert Gellately, *Backing Hitler: Consent and Coercion in Nazi Germany* (Oxford: Oxford University Press, 2001).

Himmler speech – 'I also want to mention ... never to be mentioned': A recording of the speech, together with an English translation, can be found online at http://www.holocaust-history.org/himmler-poznan/

'While some have argued that the Shoah was the result of a distinctly German form of anti-Semitism': Daniel Goldhagen, *Hitler's Willing Executioners: Ordinary Germans and the Holocaust* (London: Abacus, 1997).

'Given this knowledge, it has been argued that the Allies could have intervened militarily to stop or hinder the killings': David S. Wyman, *The Abandonment of the Jews: America and the Holocaust, 1941–1945* (New York: New Press, 2007).

A Jewish joke: From Steve Lipman, *Laughter in Hell: The Use of Humor during the Holocaust* (Lanham, MD: Jason Aronso, 1993), p. 180.

'Some historians have argued that in Israel, as well as in Zionist circles worldwide, the Shoah was at first almost a taboo, an embarrassment': See, for example: Tom Segev, *The Seventh Million: The Israelis and the Holocaust* (New York: Owl Books, 1991).

'it has been argued that we are witnessing the rise of the "new anti-Semitism"': Paul Iganski and Barry Kosmin, *The New Antisemitism? Debating Judeophobia in 21st-century Britain* (London: Profile Books, 2003).

'Jean-Paul Sartre argued that anti-Semitism defined Jews to such an extent that Jewish identity was essentially an artefact of anti-Semitism': Jean-Paul Sartre, *Anti-Semite and Jew: An Exploration of the Etiology of Hate* (New York: Schocken Books, 1995).

'Some have gone further and argued that Jews have at times "internalized" anti-Semitism as "selfhatred", seeing oneself and one's fellow Jews as anti-Semites see them': Sander L. Gilman, *Jewish Self-Hatred: Anti-Semitism and the Hidden Language of the Jews* (Baltimore, MD: John Hopkins University Press, 1990).

'Emile Fackenheim famously argued that the "614th commandment" (traditionally, there are seen to be 613 in the Bible) was "Thou shalt not give Hitler a posthumous victory"': Emile Fackenheim, *The Jewish Return into History: Reflections in the Age of Auschwitz and a New Jerusalem* (New York: Schocken Books, 1978), pp. 23–4.

Chapter 9

'Those Israelis who were born in the country – nicknamed sabras – have no memories of Jewish life outside the state of Israel': Named after a thorny desert fruit – prickly on the outside but sweet inside.

Chapter 10

'The writer Simon Rawidowicz once described the Jews as "the ever dying people"': Simon Rawidowicz, 'Israel: The Ever Dying People', in *Studies in Jewish Thought* (Philadelphia: Jewish Publication Society of America, 1974), pp. 210–24.

'A US survey published in 1991 showed that more than 50 per cent of Jews were marrying non-Jews': Barry Kosmin et al., *Highlights of the CJF 1990 National Jewish Population Survey* (New York: Council of Jewish Federations, 1991).

'The world Jewish population, currently around 13.5 million is growing slowly, at 0.6 per cent per year': 'Number of Jews in the world with emphasis on the United States and Israel', The Jewish People Policy Institute, 2011, online at http://jppi.org.il/uploads/Number_of_Jews_in_the_world_with_emphasis_on_the_United_States_and_Israel_EN.pdf

'In the UK, for example, the 20 to 40,000-strong Haredi population (numbers are disputed) is growing at the rate of at least 4 per cent a year': Daniel Vulkan and David Graham, *Population Trends among Britain's Strictly Orthodox Jews* (London: Board of Deputies of British Jews, June 2008).

'The historian Bernard Wasserstein has argued that Jews will eventually vanish from Europe, outside some pockets of Haredim': Bernard Wasserstein, *Vanishing Diaspora: The Jews in Europe since 1945* (London: Penguin, 1996).

'Israel is the world's largest Jewish population, with about 5.75 million Jews, with the US coming second at around 5.2 million': http://www.cbs.gov.il/shnaton61/st02_27.pdf

'In the UK one study found that in 1997 there were more than 2,000 Jewish organizations in the UK, with a combined income of more than £500 million': Peter Halfpenny and Margaret Reid, *The Financial Resources of the UK Jewish Voluntary Sector* (London: Institute for Jewish Policy Research, 2000).

'One study suggests that Jews make up 23 per cent of Nobel Prize winners and are similarly disproportionately represented in many other lists of high achievers': Steven L. Pease, *The Golden Age of Jewish Achievement* (Sonoma, CA: Deucalion, 2009).

'While of higher status than black Americans, they had not yet achieved the privileged status of "whiteness" they were to attain later in the 20th century': Karen Brodkin, *How Jews Became White Folks and What That Says about Race in America* (New Brunswick, NJ: Rutgers University Press, 1998).

'More recently, there has been talk of a "new Jewish culture", produced by "cool Jews", which playfully and unabashedly draws on Jewish themes in often irreverent ways': One of the articles that kicked this trend off was Joanna Smith Rakoff's 'The New Super Jews', *Time Out New York*, 4 Dec. 2003.

Term 'goyish': Goyish is a mildly pejorative Yiddish word meaning 'non-Jewish'.

'If you live in New York ... Arthur Schindler from Kiaamesha, New York' quote: Quoted in William Novak and Moshe Waldoks (eds), *The Big Book of Jewish Humor* (New York: Harper and Row, 1981), p. 60.

'Many Jews take delight in "outing" Jewish public figures and compiling lists of famous people with Jewish origins':See, for example: Guy Oseary, *Jews Who Rock* (New York: St Martin's Griffin, 2001).

100 Ideas

Maimonides' Thirteen Articles of Faith: The version given here is from *The Authorised Daily Prayer Book of the United Hebrew Congregations of the Commonwealth*, 3rd revised edn, based on a translation by Simeon Singer (Singer's Prayer Book Publication Committee, 1990), pp. 154–6.

'1 extraordinary passage from the Talmud': From Babylonian Talmud Baba Metsia 84a. Quoted in Daniel Boyarin, *Carnal Israel: Reading Sex in Talmudic Culture* (Berkeley, CA: University of California Press, 1993), p. 197.

Acknowledgements

In writing this book I have benefited from the guidance of the many Jewish teachers teachers I have encountered over the years. I am particularly grateful to Rabbi Dr Charles Middleburgh for his suggestions of books to include in the '100 Ideas' section. Most of all, I cannot even begin to quantify how much I have learned from my wife, Rabbi Dr Deborah Kahn-Harris – the finest teacher I know.

Picture credits

The author and publishers would like to thank the following for their permission to reproduce photos in this book:

Chapter 1: © Ekaterina Lin – Fotolia; **Chapter 2:** © Israel images/Alamy; **Chapter 3:** © ParisSharing/http://www.flickr.com/photos/parisharing/6809697056/sizes/o/in/photostream/http://creativecommons.org/licenses/by/2.0/; **Chapter 4:** © Jennie Faber/http://www.flickr.com/photos/jenniewoo/3439285776/sizes/o/in/photostream/http://creativecommons.org/licenses/by/2.0/; **Chapter 5:** © The Art Gallery Collection/Alamy; **Chapter 6:** © SVLuma – Fotolia; **Chapter 7:** © Library of Congress, Prints & Photographs Division, Bain Collection (LC-DIG-ggbain-17080); **Chapter 8:** © World History Archive/TopFoto **Chapter 9:** Ben Gurion declaring independence of state of Israel © Bettmann/Corbis; Eli Valley cartoon © Eli Valley www.evcomics.com; **Chapter 10:** © Startraks Photo/Rex Features.

Index

Abraham 14
academia 56
adaptation 51–2
alcohol 125
Am Yisrael Chai (song) 138
Amidah 31
Anglo-Jewry 140–41
anti-imperialism 67
anti-Semitism 50–51, 54, 74–8, 79–82, 93–6
  books on 132–3
  Muslim 78–9
  Nazi 84–93
annual festivals 24–7
Arafat, Yasser 106
Aramaic 20
Ark of the Covenant 13
Ashkenazi Jews 47–8
assimilation 54–5, 116, 121–3

Babylonian Talmud 20–22
Balfour, Arthur 70
Bar/Bat mitzvah 27
Baron-Cohen, Sasha 120, 141
Basle Programme 69
beards 37
beliefs 40–42
Ben-Gurion, David 100–101
Ben-Yehuda, Eliezer 71
blogs 137
blood libels 75, 77
Board of Deputies 64
Bolsheviks 65–6
books 16–19
boundaries 34–40
Bratt, Harvey 140–41
Brit (covenant) 14
Brit milah 27

British Jews 118
Bruce, Lenny 124–5
Bundism 66–7
burial 28
businessmen 121

Carlebach, Shlomo 138
Carmelli's bakery 141
celebrated Jews 119–24, 140–41
ceremonies 27–8
Chanukah 25–6
Christianity 74–5, 77
Chupah 27–8
civil rights 53
clothing 36–7
comedy 123
comics 124
Commentary journal 72
communism 66
communities 37–8, 51, 116, 118
  in unusual places 139–40
concentration camps 87
conscription 104, 109
Conservative Jews 63–4, 71–2
conversion to Judaism 4, 38–9, 47
culture, books on 135–6
Curaçao, Jews in 139

Damascus Affair 79
death 28, 31
defining Jews 3–4
denial of the Holocaust 93–4
Deutscher, Isaac 54–5
Diaspora 46–56, 70, 110–13
  books on 131–2
Dreyfus, Alfred 80–82

ALL THAT MATTERS: JUDAISM

Edward I of England 76
Eichmann, Adolf 92–3
Elswood, Mrs 140
emancipation 52–4, 65
endogamy 34
Enlightenment 52–3
entertainment industry 121–4

facial hair 37
Fackenheim, Emile 96
falafel 110
Fateless (film, 2005) 138
festivals 25–7
fiction 136–7
films 137–8
Finland, Jews in 139
food 34–5, 110, 125
France, Jewish emancipation in 53–4
Frank, Anne 92
Friedman, Debbie 139
fundamentalism 41
future of Judaism 116–17

Gemara 17–18
ghettoes 86, 90–91
God 13–14, 41
good and evil 15
government in Israel 103–4

halachah 22
Haredi Jews 58–61, 109, 117
Haskalah 53
hats 37
Hebrew (language) 20, 70–71, 98–9
Hebrew Bible 10–12, 16–17
Herzl, Theodor 69
Heschel, Abraham Joshua 24, 67
Hillel 10
Himmler, Heinrich 89
Hirsch, Samson Raphael 61
Hitler, Adolf 84, 85

history 10–12
    books on 131–2
Hollywood 121–2
Holocaust (*Shoah*) 84, 86–94, 96
    books on 132–3
homosexuality 38, 64

identity 36–8, 54–5
immigration to Israel 102
integration 55, 121–2
Iran, Jews in 140
Israel 94–5, 98–108
    books on 133–4
    modern 108–13

Jazz Singer, The (film, 1927) 122, 137
Jerusalem 101
Jesus' death, absolution for 77
'Jew', origin of the word 4
'Jewishness' 3–4, 124–6
jobs 49, 55–6
jokes 5

Kabbalah 19
Kaddish 31
kashrut 34–5
Kastner, Rodolf 91
Keeping the Faith (film, 2000) 138
Ketuvim 17
Knessets 103–4
Kol Nidre (song) 138
Kook, Abraham Isaac 'Rav' 61
kosher food 34–5

Ladino 48
languages 20, 47–8, 70–71, 98–9,
    118, 141
laws, anti-Semitic 85
Lemba Jews, Africa 140
Levi, Primo 92
liberalism 67–8

life, preservation of 15
lifestyle, books on 134–5
Limmud conference 118
literature 136–7
Luxembourg, Rosa 68

Maimonedes 40, 142–3
mamzerim 39
Marr, Wilhelm 74
marriage 27–8, 34, 39, 109
Mehadrin Rhyming (song) 139
Messiah 15, 40–41
Midrash 19
milestones 27–8
military in Israel 104
minyan 32
Mishnah 17–18
Mitnagdic Jews 58
mitzvot 22
Mizrachi Jews 48
modesty in dress 36
monotheism 13
Montefiore, Moses 64
mourning 28, 31
music 123, 138–9
Muslim anti-Semitism 78–9, 94

Naqba 101–2
Nazism 84–93
Neturi Karta sect 61
Neviim 16–17
New Left 67, 72
Noachide Laws 14
Nordau, Max 70
Not by Might (song) 139
novels 136–7

Obama, Barak 67–8
'one-state solution' 107
Orphaned Land 139
Orthodoxy 58–62

Oslo Accords 106
Ottoman Empire 69

Palestine 68–71, 98–102
Palestinian Arabs 100–103, 106–7, 108
Palestinian Liberation Organization
    (PLO) 105–6
Palwin 140
persecution 75–6, 80, 85–95
Pesach 26
philosophy, books on 128–30
Pikuach Nefesh 15
Pittsburgh Platform 62–3
pogroms 79, 85
politics 64–8
population change 116–17
practices, books on 130–31
practices in common 42–3
prayers 24, 29–32
Prince of Egypt, The (film, 1998) 138
Protestantism 76–7
Protocols of the Elders of Zion, The
    81–2
Purim 26

rabbis 39–40
Rabin, Yitzhak 106
radicalism 65–7
Rawidowicz, Simon 116
Rebbe, The 60
Reform Jews 62–4
remembrance 92–3, 96
Responsa 19
Rosh Chodesh 24
Rosh Hashanah 25
Rothschild, Lionel de 53
Rothschild dynasty 56
Russian Empire 77

Sacks, Jonathan 116
Sapari (song) 139

Sartre, Jean-Paul 95
Schindler, Oskar 90
Second World War 85–93
secularism 108–9, 111
Sephardi Jews 48
services 30–32
settlements 105
sexuality 34, 38, 64
Shabbat (Sabbath) 24, 34
Shanghai, Jews in 139–40
shatnez 37
Shavuot 26
Shema 30–31, 36–7
Shoah (Holocaust) 84, 86–94, 96
books on 132–3
shtetis 47
Simchat bat 27
Simchat Torah 25
Six Day War (1967) 104
Sofer, Moses 58
songs 138–9
Spinoza, Baruch 52
story of Judaism 10–12
success 55–6, 119–24
Sukkot 25
superpower, Israel as 104–5
synagogues 32

tallit 36
Talmud 10, 17–19, 21–2, 51, 143–4
Tanakh 16–17
tefillin 36–7
Temple in Jerusalem 11–13

territories, control of 104–5
terrorism 100, 105
texts, books on 127–8
theology, books on 128–30
Thirteen Principles of Faith 40,
    142–3
time 24–8
Tisha B'Av 26
Torah 16, 20–22, 31
    scroll 29
trade unions 66
'two-state solution' 106–7
Tzedakah 15
tzitzit 36

universalism 15
Ushpizin (film, 2005) 137–8
USSR 65–6

Wagner, Richard 81
wars with Israel 104–5
Wasserstein, Bernard 117
wine 140

Y-Love 139
Yiddish 47–8, 118, 141
Yishuv 98–100
Yisreal 4
Yochanan, Rabbi 143–4
Yom Kippur 25, 111

Zionism 61, 68–71, 98–102, 110–11
    books on 133–4